Surviving the Classroom Observation

A handbook for trainee teachers in Education & Training

Copyright © 2016 Darren Purdie

All rights reserved.

ISBN-13: 978-1535331784

ISBN-10: 153533178X

Copyright © 2016 Darren Purdie

The right of Darren Purdie to be identified as the author of this work has been asserted by him in accordance with sections 77 and 78 of the Copyright, Designs and Patents Act 1988.

All rights reserved. This book or any portion thereof may not be reprinted, reproduced or utilised in any form or by any electronic, mechanical, or other means, now known or hereafter invented, including photocopying and recording, or in any information storage or retrieval systems, without the express written permission of the publisher except for the use of brief quotations in a book review or scholarly journal.

Trademark notice: product or corporate names may be trademarks or registered trademarks, and are used only for identification and explanation without intent to infringe.

About The Book

This Handbook is designed for those trainee teachers undertaking their Diploma in Education & Training, but is also suitable for those completing other similar qualifications. The purpose is to demystify the formally assessed classroom observations, as well as provide useful strategies for trainee teachers to adopt that will support their work prior to, during, and after their assessed sessions.

About The Author

Darren Purdie has worked within education for over 20 years. Originally specialising in professional performing arts training, Darren was soon drawn into the wider world of post-compulsory education and training, and has subsequently worked in a number of strategic positions; initially curriculum development and management, then into quality leadership roles. The pursuit and development of quality education is one of Darren's core values, and throughout his management career, he has always maintained his teaching status, believing that if a manager is to give credible feedback, that manager should have practical experience of the modern day classroom.

Darren is currently the Quality & Curriculum Manager in a London college. He continues to work as an Ofsted inspector (a role he has held for over 15 years), and as a consultant, supporting the quality initiatives and curriculum reviews of Further Education colleges nationwide. Darren directly manages and continues to develop and deliver a range of teacher training programmes, including the Diploma and Certificate in Education and Training. He was one of the consultants who worked with Standards Verification UK (SVUK) in the supporting of awarding institutions and universities during the transition to the revised teaching qualifications following the 2007 reforms. Darren has developed and delivered observation training programmes to observers (and teachers), and this work was central to his doctoral studies.

CONTENTS

Acknowledgments   I

Introduction

1   The Changing Face of Teacher Training   1

2   Understanding Observation as Assessment   Pg 25

3   Planning, Planning, Planning   Pg 43

4   Learning, Learning, Learning   Pg 75

5   Assessment: Monitoring, Tracking & Using   Pg 117

6   Reflection as Action   Pg 149

7   One Step Closer   Pg 165

    Bibliography   Pg 169

ACKNOWLEDGMENTS

This handbook is dedicated to all of those trainee teachers I have had the privilege of working with; watching them all grow and develop as professionals, finding their own styles and experimenting bravely with new ideas and approaches. They all survived their classroom observations and, in many cases, have gone on to achieve great things with their own learners. Similarly, I'd very much like to thank those trainee teachers who so willingly contributed their insights and experiences to me whilst researching aspects of this book – your words have been touching, thought-provoking and, at times, inspirational.

I also must recognise the wonderful work done by so many classroom observers who tirelessly roam institutions and organisations, squeeze into tight corners trying to be as invisible as they can, whilst balancing their laptops with teacher folders and learners' work; all whilst attentively observing the teaching and learning. Observees find the process challenging, but let us not ever forget it can be a challenge on both sides at times. Your perseverance and determination to support and nurture the best in education and training is commendable, and so often under-appreciated. Well, not today. Today, it is appreciated so very much indeed.

Lastly, on a personal level, I want to thank Ann Lahiff and Ken Spours for steering me, Matt O'Leary for re-invigorating me, and my family and friends for never abandoning me. This wouldn't be here without you.

Darren Purdie

Introduction

Tests are scary.

Well, to many people they are. All too often, teacher-educators forget that the teaching qualifications for those working in the post-compulsory sector test the skills and knowledge of their trainee teachers in several ways. Yes, there is a range of challenging assignments, asking you to explore and engage with theories, models and principles of teaching, learning and assessment and yes, you'll be exposed (one hopes) to a dazzling range of exciting and engaging activities as the course teacher works wonders to demonstrate the very best practice. But this is only part of the picture.

Your own teaching naturally generates a lot of the material you'll be using throughout your teacher training course; product evidence such as session plans, assessment records, adapted resources and so forth, but more than this, it shows your own delivery skills, and allows you the opportunity to engage in a professional discussion with your assessor regarding your own development. Admittedly, this discussion may well take many forms depending where you undertake your training, but one aspect of this is constant – you will receive feedback. That feedback is an important clue to the oft-overlooked reality – these observations are ***tests***.

Rarely openly acknowledged, the purpose of this part of the

course is to test your teaching skills in action. Naturally, there are some clear criteria which are set and must be observed; indeed, in recent years, some awarding institutions for teacher training have adopted – somewhat controversially – a grading system reminiscent of previous inspection regimes implemented by Ofsted. This is a topic for discussion later in the book, but whether one likes it or not, it is there with the intention of supporting teachers to develop and improve.

So, you ask, am I saying that these observations are a form of assessment for learning? Well, I reply, I may well be. But not solely that – one hopes that they also demonstrate sufficient coverage to be a valid means by which to infer assessment of learning as well (and at the very least). Chapter Two will explore this in more detail, and go some way towards supporting a trainee teacher in how best to approach this form of testing. Let's not forget, after all, that tests are scary.

Am I trying to instil fear into you? Not at all! I am, however, recognising that these assessed observations can be unnerving. They can make you worry. For those undertaking in-service training, this might very well be the first ever experience of a formal classroom observation. Teachers can develop classroom performance anxiety. And if that happens, if you are someone who finds yourself poring over your session plan to check you've been explicit, to ensure you've got some seamlessly adapted resources ready so that all the learners can join in without a whiff of non-inclusive practice in the air, and if you are someone who wants to be absolutely sure that every participant in that room can contribute and achieve, then congratulations – you've already passed the first test. You've shown that you care.

The role of a teacher has, over the years, had a lot of mixed press. When national league tables are down, it's the teachers' fault. When everyone is getting A grades in their exams, well – obviously the exams are too easy (it couldn't possibly be the teachers doing a spectacular job, now could it?). Government priorities shift and the focus of external inspectorates gently steer organisational policy which – let's be honest – tends to manifest as more paperwork. Well, that's how it can feel, at least. I know, as I'm in the interesting position of being both an instigator and a do-er in this playground we call education, and I see some teachers engage with gusto and others, less so.

The role is challenging, and the role is demanding. It quite often demands more than the time allotted to complete it allows, and so many dedicated professionals, and trainee professionals, continue to rise to the challenge and go that extra mile. Is it right that they should have to? That's a discussion for another day, but it is what a great teacher does. Because, like you, they *care*.

This book isn't designed to make you a great teacher overnight, so sorry if I just dashed your expectations. Nor will it tell you how to pass all of your written assignments for your courses. There are many, many wonderful and fascinating books on how best to grapple with your written work. There are also some dull ones. This aims to be neither of these – that is frankly the last thing the world needs. No, this book will mostly be focusing upon the observations. It may well, by necessity, straddle some other aspects of your work but I make no apology for that. Quite the opposite, as I hope you will be able to see connections between what the theoretical elements of the course demand of you intellectually, and what the practical classroom assessments expect of you professionally.

We will look together at the Professional Standards for Teachers and Trainers in Education and Training, and throughout the book connections will be made between that which is asked of you in your planning and delivery, and these standards. Each chapter will build up your personal knowledge around key aspects of the observation, from its origins in teacher-training policy through time, to how it actually works as an assessment tool.

Following this, the core observation criteria will be broken down into the planning phase, and the teaching and learning phase to make grappling with, and preparing for, the observations that much easier. Additionally, you'll find a few 'Reality Check' points throughout the chapters. These are to prompt some personal reflection and possible discussion, but you may also spot that they link to key parts of the theoretical elements of your course work. So don't disregard them; they may help you make some meaningful links between the theory and the practice.

The rest of the book is designed to help you focus on yourself, your strengths and areas for development; these are not set in stone, and no doubt will change as you move through your course. Similarly, this book – whilst specifically focused on supporting you with your formally assessed observations – does have an extended shelf life for you too; once you are working regularly as a teacher, being observed as part of quality assurance and quality improvement measures will become a recurring feature. It is hoped sincerely that many of the skills that you can grow through using this book can be readily transferred into any observation.

This isn't an easy career, but I suspect you know that already. It is rewarding, and it can be frustrating in equal measure. All the intellectual skill in the world will not always be enough to help you survive in the classroom. I doubt the book could ever be written that can help you to address every eventuality you'll encounter (there will be many you'll never forget, and a few that other people may never believe). I am hopeful, drawing on more years that I can actually believe, that the experiences and suggestions, the strategies and the points for consideration that I present for you in this book will help you feel confident moving forwards, both in your numerous assessed classroom sessions, but also beyond into your worthwhile and well earned career. As any great teacher knows, preparation is the key.

Maybe, if you're well prepared for them, tests aren't so scary after all.

Surviving The Classroom Observation

1 THE CHANGING FACE OF TEACHER TRAINING

This Chapter will put the current approach to post-compulsory education and training into context for trainees, and provide a brief but considered historical reflection on the way both the qualifications, and the professional status and recognition of teachers in the sector, has developed, including the introduction of the assessed observed teaching practice. This also sets the historical policy context of teaching as a profession, including the present Professional Standards, as defined by the Education & Training Foundation, which may support aspects of your written assignments.

This Chapter relates to the following Professional Standards:

Professional values and attributes *– (2) Evaluate and challenge your practice, values and beliefs*

Professional knowledge and understanding *– (8) Maintain and update your knowledge of educational research to develop evidence-based practice; (12) Understand the teaching and professional role and your responsibilities*

Professional skills *– (19) Maintain and update your teaching and learning expertise and vocational skills through collaboration with employers; (20) Contribute to organisational* *development and quality improvement through collaboration with others.*

Admittedly, no one is reading this book for a history lesson. However, all too often, trainee teachers are left ill informed of the legacy that stretches out behind them. This is particularly true of those working in what is broadly termed "post-compulsory education and training" (PCET). The term itself is something of a non-sequitur these days, as relatively recent reforms to the English education structure has raised the participation age for pupils from 16 years to 18 years, thus placing 'Further Education' (FE), which has long been considered a core component of the PCET stable, squarely within the traditional compulsory education bracket.

An emerging umbrella term for those attending education outside of the previously traditional age bracket is that of the 'Learning and Skills Sector.' The term is born of policy initiatives and the associated focusing (and re-focusing) of seemingly ever diminishing public money to prioritise and support those aspects of on-going training that can actively support economic growth, and possible community cohesion, within 21st century British society.

This is not going to be news for you, as the struggle between instrumentalist and liberal humanist philosophies within education is sure to raise its head on your programme. The notion of the government of the time (irrespective of *which* time) setting the agenda around what the country does or doesn't value in terms of qualifications or educational pathways is hardly new, and is a useful link to begin this brief exploration down memory lane.

The value of initial teacher education for teachers in the Learning & Skills Sector (including Adult and Community Education) has long been a very mixed picture.

Whilst it is going back a bit, we can see from the Russell Report (1966) that of those actively working in FE, and then technical colleges within the late 1960s, less than one third had gained – or engaged in – any type of formal teacher training.

Interestingly, the findings of Cantor and Roberts (1986) indicate that in the 1970s many of the (then) Local Education Authorities (LEAs), which were responsible for the management of FE colleges at this time, were unwilling to allow the teaching staff the opportunity to attend formal teacher training. The reason given was that it would be at the expense of delivering their existing classes. Indeed, literature informs us that the only 'staff development' opportunities provided by the LEAs were external courses that would allow the teachers to maintain and update their expertise within their own curriculum specialism (Castling, 1996).

Over a decade later, the Foster Report (2005) made the observation that the Government was making changes to develop "world class teaching" whilst recognising that *"improving teaching and learning is also about subject relevance"* (2005: 33). Does this mean that policy development at both national and local level was about to come full circle? Not really, and indeed, once we see how things are in the early part of the 21st century, we can see exactly how far things have come for teachers.

In order to first put the present demands being placed upon teachers in the sector into perspective, we must consider the path taken that brought us to the current requirements for initial teacher education. Whilst I'm focusing here on developments from the 1960s it is important to recognise firstly the view of the McNair Report (1944), which found that teaching in the sector was, generally, *"dull."* The chair of the committee, Sir Andrew McNair, expressed the view that whilst both subject expertise and vocational experience were naturally of significant importance for teachers in the sector, "they were not in themselves a qualification for teaching," (Lucas 2004). This was perhaps the first time the notion of a dual professionalism was mooted within the sector, which is again a theme within your own teacher-training programme.

> **REALITY CHECK:**
>
> **Do you think holding a 'dual professionalism' is really a help or a hindrance for teachers in the Learning & Skills Sector?**
>
> **i)** **Consider your own circumstances – do you bring another professionalism to the table? How often do you rely upon it to support your teaching?** *a lot*
>
> **ii)** **Draw up a list of pros and cons for being a 'dual professional' – does one outweigh the other? Why?**

Back to McNair, and this is a stark contrast to the historical tradition of FE, which found such qualities to be perfectly acceptable, if not desirable. Indeed, the pervading notion was that many of the teachers in further education themselves considered their role as one of practitioners with specialist knowledge who were employed to teach, over the idea that they were, in fact, professional teachers (Gleeson and Mardle, 1980; Young et al, 1995; Guile and Lucas, 1999).

This is a popular argument, and many teachers engaged in the sector today, particularly with vocational backgrounds, would argue the benefits to the learners of these attributes. It is undeniable that these qualities are far more than just desirable, but as this report illustrates so clearly, this is not quite enough.

The McNair Report is a contribution to the literature worth mentioning, because it is also the first of its kind to publicly acknowledge that there should be no distinction between a teacher of further education (or in this context, teachers working in technical colleges) and one from any other sector. The significance of this will become clear a little later in this chapter, but is something so few trainees are necessarily aware of, and given the curiously ever fluctuating approach to licensing teachers in the Learning & Skills Sector, an awareness of our history may well equip us better for the future.

By the eve of the 1960s very little had changed significantly. The White Paper of 1956 entitled 'Technical Education' prompted the Willis Jackson Report of the following year. This identified an estimated 51,000 teachers in the sector, 40,000 of which were part time (MoE, 1957). There were, at this time, only 300 places available at the existing three dedicated FE teacher-training colleges.

The findings of the Willis Jackson Report demonstrated that two-thirds of the actual delivery taking place at the technical colleges was by the full-time staff, and of these full time teachers, only **one third** had actually engaged in formal teacher training. The inclusion of the substantial number of part time teachers impacts significantly on these statistics, meaning only **one fifth** of the courses on offer were being delivered by 'qualified' teachers (MoE 1957). The Crowther Report (1959) made the recommendation that opportunities for expansion with regard to teacher training in the FE sector be introduced and this led, amongst other things, to the introduction of the fourth teacher training college in Wolverhampton.

The Crowther Report concluded that 75 per cent of newly appointed teachers had not been in receipt of formalised initial teacher education and given that the projected growth of the teaching population was estimated at 8000 more part time and 7000 more full time FE teachers by 1961 these were figures that merited concern. Certainly, it raises questions as to how effective these teachers were – were they merely reciting their own knowledge or were they actually delivering a learning experience? Bristow (1970), a college principal, observed that the teaching in FE was *"extremely pedestrian and uninspired...there was no participation."* Bristow pointed out that, in his personal view, the teachers would opt to lecture in the most literal sense or, in more extreme instances, *"read directly from the textbook"* (1970:53)

It is not until the arrival of the Russell Report (1966) that the first suggestion of mandatory teacher training was suggested. The report found that two thirds of the technical and FE College teaching body were still not formally trained. The recommendation of the report was relatively visionary, stating as it did that their suggestion was all new teachers in this sector should engage in teacher training within three years of being employed. Today, we might find that less surprising – indeed, the surprise is more likely to be the lax approach of colleges to seeing trained and qualified teachers as central to their quality assurance policy. But at this point in our history, looking after teachers as a professional body just simply wasn't deemed relevant.

This visionary recommendation, to be implemented by all Local Education Authorities (LEAs) by 1969 was dismissed by the Secretary of State (Lucas, 2004), preferring instead to maintain the voluntary system but with a concession that some new incentives to undertake such training be made available. These incentives consisted of secondments and increases in salary depending on gaining formally, recognised teacher training (Bratchell 1968).

The Crowther Report also made an interesting observation that one issue with the training of FE teachers was the lack of any formal qualified teacher status, a situation that has remained until very recently, in the scheme of things. However, the Crowther Report found that establishing such a recognised status was not possible in the technical and FE college arena (1966). This is a notable divergence from current thinking, where such a qualification status was finally in development as a part of the reform (DfES 2003) to bring FE teachers' status into alignment with that of secondary and primary teachers, and finally became a live concept in 2007. Therefore, whilst the recommendations of the Crowther Report were visionary, the foresight was lacking some of the wisdom of McNair from 22 years earlier.

It was not until the James Report (1972) that the value of pre-service and in-service initial teacher education (ITE) gained a degree of prominence (Guile & Lucas, 1999). Set up by the then Secretary of State at the Department of Education and Science, Margaret Thatcher, the James Committee – following its enquiries into teacher training – recommended that further education teachers follow a "Three-Cycle" system (Lucas, 2004). This system made assumptions on the existing experience of the teachers, and whilst many of its recommendations were not taken forward, the suggestion that opportunities for increased participation in ITE be made available was more warmly embraced.

It is interesting to note here the repetition that occurs so frequently in the findings of the many committees and reports of this time. All those charged with the investigation of ITE return with very similar findings, that too few teachers are engaging with formal training and that colleges' governance are placing too much reliance on the teachers' natural ability to transmit their own considerable subject specific expertise to their expectant learners. At no point do we find any reference, in official terms, to the quality of the classroom experience. How much value was given to this factor? Not much at this point, it seems. This was, however, the all too familiar pattern with further education overall. As Lucas (2004) calls it, the FE sector was indeed struggling to evolve through a *"history of neglect."*

In keeping with this tradition of insignificance so often attributed historically to FE, and given the range of economical and political upheavals taking place in the early 1970s, the proposals made by the James Report were put on hold. This was not, however, the end. In their stead, October 1973 saw the arrival of the Advisory Committee on the Supply and Training of Teachers (ACSETT). Emerging from this was the first of three key publications that became known as the Haycocks reports.

Haycocks 1 (DES 1975) put forward proposals for the training of full-time teachers. One key proposal was the introduction of a target of 5 per cent of the full-time teaching staff from any individual FE college should be engaged on an in-service training programme, of a day release nature, providing the course itself was recognised (Lucas, 2004). Despite the Department of Education and Science supporting the proposals, the lack of funding again impacted upon the sector's development and the target was reduced to 3 per cent.

The second report was published in 1978 and this time focused, finally, on the need to train the part time staff in FE colleges. Haycocks 2 promoted the case that the inconsistency that prevailed in the sectors' teacher training needed to be tamed, in the absence of a sector specific regulatory body. The major proposal from the second report was the development of a three-stage teaching qualification to meet the needs of part time tutors. It was noted that some of the part time teachers did hold the 730 certification from the City and Guilds of London Institute. A few had Royal Society of Arts (RSA) or College of Preceptors qualifications (Foden 1992).

Haycocks 3 (1978) was a discussion paper on the training of teachers in the adult education arena in preparation for management. Sadly, no real heed was taken of the steer these reports offered. Certainly, it can be said that these reports were once again visionary, but, once again, the tradition of marginalising FE was upheld. Foden comments on the "remarkable" quality of these reports (1992) observing that it was rare for government funded bodies to fly so clearly in the face of existing policy. Whilst not fully embraced by government, the reports carried significant influence in the increased participation of further education tutors with teacher training across the remainder of the 70s and the 1980s.

Leading up to the incorporation of further education colleges in 1993, the mantle of responsibility for providing initial teacher education lay firmly with the colleges appointing the teachers and their Local Education Authorities. Equally, there was no governance over the setting of minimum requirements for FE teachers. The variety in quality and consistency of ITE in many respects reflected the diverse and fragmented sector to which it catered.

During this period, the Department for Education and Science introduced their Grants for Educational Support and Training (GEST) fund. This was established to be administered by the LEAs to allow for budgeting of staff development. This was an initiative to regulate the hitherto uneven dispersal of FE staff training (Cantor et al, 1995). As the sector had been given leave to implement staff development without any considered structure, the time was right – as indeed numerous previous reports had indicated – for a more criterion based approach to rigorous staff training.

More institutions of Higher Education became designated during the early 1990s as providers of initial teacher education, offering the nationally recognised Certificate in Education/PGCE. Of particular interest to us, is that for the first time in this journey of development, there was an emphasis upon the observation of practical teaching; a factor that pleasingly was also present in the popular alternative ITE course, the City & Guilds 7307 Further and Adult Teacher's Certificate. Interestingly, many FE colleges now offered this qualification and, for many institutions over time this would become a minimum expectation seen as equipping the staff with all the skills needed – in generic terms – to deliver learning professionally to the post-compulsory sector. What is of particular interest here is that this award is designated as only a Level Three qualification, and did include a loose observation framework, albeit extremely flimsy. Whilst popular for so long, the honeymoon period with the 7307 was not destined to last forever.

The final approach to the present day followed the Government's incorporation of further education colleges. The links that had been so long established between the LEAs, the colleges and the national staff training budgets were deconstructed (Spours & Lucas, 1996). The Further Education Funding Council (FEFC) was quick to avoid responsibility for the monitoring of ITE, and placed the onus for this – including the local investment in teaching staff – firmly with the individual colleges. With no national communication or common scaffolding upon which to set clear and consistent targets it is hardly surprising that again the sector moved forward spasmodically with no strategic direction.

Ironically, the FEFC cited in a report (1999) that a significantly low proportion of colleges had *"...given priority to the development of effective teaching skills even when lesson inspection grades revealed pedagogic weaknesses."* The FEFC in this report went on to comment that there was too little investment in staff development *"in a sector that should believe in the benefits of training"* but where they had done nothing as a body to promote such action.

A positive impact in the late nineties was the Training and Development Lead Body's (TDLB) introduction of the Common Accords (Lucas, 2004). These accords provided commonality for the first time across the primary awarding bodies (such as City and Guilds). This contributed hugely to the standardisation of assessing in ITE.

It was the incoming Labour government of 1997 who introduced a series of National Training Organisations (NTOs), one of which was charged specifically with Further Education. A key function of this body was that of defining occupational standards that would be recognised on a national level. Exactly how effective FENTO actually was is debatable. It is true that the introduction in January 1999 of the FENTO standards in initial teacher education (Armitage et al, 2003) provided a tangible benchmark for those providers of ITE. However, representative of the sector's historical commitment to development Lucas (2004) tells us that FE employers were heavily underrepresented at FENTO meetings.

This raises the issue of perception. Many teachers working within FE have often mirrored the words of McNair (1944) in seeking parity with those teachers working in the formative stages of general education, yet once more the seeming disinterest in actively engaging with change emanating from the sector itself more clearly reflects the narrow view expressed in the Crowther report (1966) — without commitment from the sector how can it be possible to achieve a consistent level of status equivalent to those in the compulsory sector? Not until the dawn of the twenty first century do we see in the new reforms what, in principle at least, has the makings of a solid framework for the regulation and standardisation of initial teacher education.

In the consultation paper "Learning to Succeed" (DfEE, 2000), the same Labour government highlighted their focus on the improvement of post-compulsory tuition, in particular the raising of standards within the quality of the teaching and learning. After debate, the Statutory Instrument 1209 (2001), was introduced enforcing mandatory ITE for all FE tutors who, to date, lacked recognised qualifications. To be clear, however, this did not yet extend to include those delivering within Adult & Community Learning providers, or Higher Education.

This development was linked to the emergent FENTO standards introduced earlier. Awarding bodies, such as City and Guilds, now faced the need for FENTO endorsement – did their qualifications meet these new standards? If so,

REALITY CHECK:

Much time has passed since the 1990s saw such a focus on the development of FE teachers, but how far has the political landscape shifted?

  i) To support you in your studies, and also to keep you up to date with important educational matters, explore current educational policy at national level.
  ii) Can you see any political traits that duplicate any of these proposals from the past? Are there any new and exciting innovations that are noteworthy?

endorsement was granted. Where possible, providers of the PGCE/Cert.Ed merely mapped existing programmes across to the new standards (Lucas 2004). In order to meet the higher demands, City and Guilds introduced a new qualification for Further and Adult teachers designated the 7407. This was a level four award, and the demands placed upon candidates were considerably greater than had previously been expected on the 7307 courses. Further implications of this will be discussed momentarily.

The inspectorate, Ofsted, was charged with undertaking a survey of the quality of this new shape of ITE, in conjunction with the Adult Learning Inspectorate, the findings of which were published in 2003. They were less than glowing. To quote the opening sentence from the overall summary:

> "The current system of FE teacher training does not provide a satisfactory foundation of professional development for FE teachers at the start of their careers." (Ofsted, 2003)

Additionally, the report was critical overall of the observational element of the training programmes, going so far as to state that the trainees' *"...progress is inhibited by insufficient observation and feedback on their teaching; observation of trainees' teaching does not have a high enough profile in their assessment"* (2003).

Whilst this survey came on the heels of the Success for All agenda (2002), it would be hard to ignore its impact on the new reforms published by the Standards Unit in July 2004 (DfES 2005), which highlighted a five year development plan for the sector.

For the first time, tangible steps were being taken to significantly raise the profile of FE teachers, and a part of the new reform would be a move towards the acquisition of a new status mark for teachers within the learning and skills sector (DfES 2005). This new award was intended to bring the oft-sought parity between the educational sectors, granting FE tutors Qualified Teacher – Learning & Skills (QTLS) status. This would be the equivalent to the Qualified Teacher Status (QTS) held by colleagues in the compulsory sector. But what would be the cost to the teachers?

The Ofsted survey (2003) recommended that awarding bodies needed to *"give substantially more attention to developing trainees' expertise in teaching"* which given their findings is not unexpected. The response produced by the Standards Unit (2005) described the new offer to trainee FE teachers as part of the reform in the document "Equipping Our Teachers for the Future." The document outlined the new pathway post-compulsory teachers could follow, which interestingly allowed for an 'early exit point' for teachers with limited roles.

The new ITE blueprint provided two routes, one was a "Passport to Teaching" the other a full "Licence to Practice" and, according to the document *"both courses will also contain elements designed to respond to Ofsted's findings"* (2005). The key fundamental components included to meet the needs of those participants are an initial assessment geared to determine the correct path for the individual; accreditation of prior learning as more experienced teachers may be able to fast-track aspects of the new course.

It also included a statutory requirement that those teachers working for providers who delivered under a publicly funded contract (such as with the Learning & Skills Council, later the Skills Funding Agency) had to be both qualified (with either the new Diploma or Certificate in Teaching in the Lifelong

Learning Sector, commonly identified as DTLLS and CTLLS respectively), but also had to be a member of the newly formed Institute for Learning (IfL). This was a professional body created to provide recognition to FE and adult education teachers. However, politics and priorities would soon show this development as built upon a shaky foundation.

This applied to all teachers in the sector; it introduced an interesting new challenge for those providing this ITE – particularly with the addition of the core curriculum assessment of literacy, language and numeracy embedded within the delivery of the ITE programmes. How are trainees themselves to successfully up-skill to the required levels? The guidance published by the DfES in October 2005 served to reinforce the stylish new reform, but upon review contains little tangible substance. Indeed, this is supported when at one point the guidance instructs Teacher Trainers and Educators to "...*check that teacher trainers are appropriately qualified and experienced...*" (DfES 2005a). This prompts some concern as to how far the scaffolding for this new initiative was actually in place, especially when the Government had set the deadline for existing teachers to enrol in suitable programmes leading to the QTLS status by September 2007. This was a target never to be met.

Certainly, the integration of core literacy and numeracy skills within the ITE programmes prompted many experienced ITE teachers within many institutions to have concerns about their own competence to deliver these new requirements. Reflecting upon the guidance offered above by the DfES, one has to wonder how widespread such concerns were. Worse still, several others felt they were too long in the tooth, or simply not 'academically minded' enough to start gaining full Level 4 or 5 qualifications, and voted with their feet. This period saw many gifted and talented teachers elect to ease themselves out of the profession. Was this always a covert and hidden agenda to trim down a sector of education that the powers that be had never seemed to be completely sure what to do with? If it was, it was a short-lived outcome.

After just a few years, the governmentally funded Institute for Learning was discovered to be too costly, as PCET teachers had – up to this point – had their memberships mostly funded by the Government (in an uncharacteristic display of real investment in the post-compulsory workforce). In line with the numerous Comprehensive Spending Reviews, this was a financial burden the country could no longer carry. The result? The Government chose not to enforce membership, and took steps to ultimately undo the significant reforms that 'Equipping Our Teachers For The Future' had brought in. Membership of the IfL was optional (and, as so few actually took this up, within a couple of years the Lingfield Report deemed it was impossible to sustain), and providers found the statutory requirement to have qualified teachers dissipated.

You could be forgiven for thinking that colleges might be pleased with this u-turn. Surely, lives were now easier? Not so. Colleges had sustained professional losses implementing these reforms; experienced teachers had departed in droves, and local policies had been devised to ensure, in many cases, a clear stance on recruiting new teachers. Furthermore, Ofsted had factors around the deployment of qualified teaching staff as a main aspect of their inspection framework. Better colleges had actually welcomed the national policy on enforced qualifications; feeling vindicated in their own locally determined and long standing commitment to having the highest standards of teaching staff.

As mentioned a little earlier, the Professional Overarching Standards developed by Lifelong Learning UK (LLUK) and Standards Verification UK (SVUK) were themselves revised early in the life of the Education & Training Foundation (the successor to the Institute for Learning). These new Professional Standards for Teachers and Trainers in Education and Training – England (2014) were significantly simplified, and in many ways far better encapsulated key aspects of the teacher role.

In their own words, the Education and & Training Foundation introduced their standards thus:

> *"Teachers and trainers are reflective and enquiring practitioners who think critically about their own educational assumptions, values and practice in the context of a changing contemporary and educational world. They draw on relevant research as part of their evidence-based practice. They act with honesty and integrity to maintain high standards of ethics and professional behaviour in support of learners and their expectations."* (ETF, 2014)

The Professional Standards themselves are broken into three key categories, all of which are designed to relate clearly to the professional role – indeed, the term 'professional' features predominately throughout the published document. The standards are presented in Table 1 both for easy reference but also to allow you to consider how many of these you demonstrate frequently as a teacher and, indeed, how many of them are demonstrated during your observed teaching practice.

Considerable emphasis is placed upon the centrality of teachers (that's you) taking ownership of their professionalism, and being active participants in the maintenance of their professional status. Is this a covert form of devolution in relation to the standards? Maybe a little, but surely it can be accepted that it should not fall to an all-seeing body alone to ensure that teachers – or indeed any profession, for that matter – are fulfilling their accountabilities and responsibilities. The phrasing of several of these standards make it clear that the onus is squarely resting on the teachers.

Table 1: Professional Standards for Teachers & Trainers (ETF, 2014)

Professional values and attributes	*Professional knowledge and understanding*	*Professional skills*
1. Reflect on what works best in your teaching and learning to meet the diverse needs of your learners 2. Evaluate and challenge your practice, values and beliefs 3. Inspire, motivate and raise aspirations of learners through your enthusiasm and knowledge 4. Be creative and innovative in selecting and adapting strategies to help learners to learn 5. Value and promote social and cultural diversity, equality of opportunity and inclusion	7. Maintain and update knowledge of your subject and/or vocational area 8. Maintain and update your knowledge of educational research to develop evidence-based practice 9. Apply theoretical understanding of effective practice in teaching, learning and assessment drawing on research and other evidence 10. Evaluate your practice with others and assess its impact on learning 11. Manage and promote positive learner behaviour 12. Understand the teaching and professional role and your responsibilities	13. Motivate and inspire learners to promote achievement and develop the skills to enable progression 14. Plan and deliver effective learning programmes for diverse groups/individuals in a safe and inclusive environment 15. Promote the benefits of technology and support learners in its use 16. Address the maths and English needs of learners and work creatively to overcome individual barriers to learning 17. Enable learners to share responsibility for their own learning

6. Build positive and collaborative relationships with colleagues and learners		and assessment, setting goals that stretch and challenge. 18. Apply appropriate and fair methods of assessment that provide constructive and timely feedback to support progression and achievement 19. Maintain and update your teaching and training expertise and vocational skills through collaboration with employers 20. Contribute to organisational development and quality improvement through collaboration with others.

Key words to reflect upon within the standards, as you progress in your studies and training, and in particular as you prepare for your observed teaching practice, are *'evaluate'*, *'update'*, *'promote'*, *'apply'* as well as the more conceptual terms requiring you to be *'innovative'* and *'creative'* in your delivery. Whilst not a short-cut to success by any means, paying attention in your own practice to the standards that use these terms will help you focus your attention moving forwards.

Even with the advent of these new, clearer standards, the removal of the national requirement for teachers in the sector to be formally qualified still left many providers facing difficult professional and strategic decisions, essentially unsupported at a political level.

Once again, the value placed upon training up teachers working in the Learning & Skills Sector faced the same kind of political and strategic apathy at a national level that had dogged and overshadowed the profession since the end of the Second World War. But this was not the biggest blow providers (and trainee teachers) would face when seeking to be the best they can be.

Under the UK's coalition government (2010-2015) many higher level, professional qualifications were taken out of the long-standing funding stable they had occupied for a number of years. The rationale for this was that those wanting to engage in higher-level education should pay for it themselves. There are arguments either way for this position, and this is not the forum for these. What is of note, and it may well be something you are acutely aware of, is that this encompassed teacher training qualifications.

2013 saw the introduction of yet another reform to the structure of the teaching qualifications, as part of a wider review that sought to align more transparently Award, Certificate and Diploma level pathways. This saw the PTLLS, DTLLS and CTLLS qualifications heavily revised and rebranded into the Award, the Certificate and the Diploma in Education and Training. Three new-look teacher-training qualifications; not one of them fundable.

So what, you cry? Well, significantly, this means to providers (the employer of teachers), they have to make a strategic choice. Option one is that they have to lower their professional standards, and not expect new teachers to become qualified (an epic degradation in terms of quality and professionalism, potentially). Option two, they require their teachers to self-fund their own qualifications (not entirely unheard of but, at a cost of between £1000-£5000, which could be off-putting to new teachers, even if they did make use of an Advanced Learning Loan).

The last option, which so few institutions are in a position to implement, is to invest heavily in their staff, and cover the cost of the qualification. This is always the most attractive option for trainees, and you may be one of the national minority, lucky enough to be in that position. Or you may have committed your own resources to pay the tuition fees. In either case, a significant investment has been made into your development in a sector of education that often sees more turbulence and change than the compulsory sector, but with much less media coverage.

How is this relevant to the observational aspects of your course? Surely *that* is what this book is all about – why am I wasting your time with this dusty old flannel? Well, my answer to that is two fold:

1. You are embarking on a journey into an exciting and challenging career, that has a long, distinguished and colourful history. Some recent educational policy-focus aside, this is an aspect of teacher training rarely explored, and it is very much my view that an appreciation of the difficulties and upheavals faced by our predecessors lends a strong perspective on what we have available to us today. You are participating in a course that countless teachers in time gone by

would hold in very high regard, not least to simply have that opportunity.

Sometimes the workload of the course can blind us to the fact that teaching is a privilege, and everything we write about and research exists because of what everyone else has gone through before us. The fact you now have access to a teaching qualification that included a focus upon your classroom practice, that includes these observations so that fellow professionals can see you in action and provide feedback is not an automatic right. It is something that, despite how we may at times feel about it, is so valuable and central to developing us as teachers, but is so often categorised as something we dread. Embrace the course, and the observations – they are an opportunity for you, not an obstacle.

2. Possibly a more prosaic response, but history is the greatest teacher of all. It is down to us to do the learning, and we have so much to learn from what has gone before. Teachers in our sector of work have fought and struggled to gain recognition, and so often this recognition of our professional standing has taken knock after knock. Even the most recent policy drivers imply an almost off-hand attitude to the status of Learning and Skills teachers. You have joined this profession; you need to know its history. As the DET course will explore, professionalism exists when there is a sense of belonging to a shared body of knowledge and experience. I'd like to contribute in some small way to your personal body of knowledge with regards to the profession you are joining. A lot of people have shaped it – I wonder how you'll contribute to shaping it in the future.

In summary, you'll now have an awareness of the rocky road those countless educationalists before you have endured to bring us to this point. You can also, I hope, begin to see just how fortunate we are to have access to such thorough and developmental qualifications that are built to provide trainees with a clear scaffolding for their professional learning. The observation of your teaching and learning in action is such an important and useful part of this, and something we tend to take for granted. Not only that, but something we might even positively dread.

This might be because you fear being watched or, worse still, judged. That's understandable, but maybe you can shift your perspective slightly? Rather than being *watched*, you're providing a chance for someone to *coach* you, based on what you've let them see. There's often more than one way to look at anything, and yes, these observations are judging your performance, but that's what we all do through assessment of our learners, isn't it? In the next chapter, we can see how to put the assessment element of the observation into context.

REALITY CHECK:

Consider your institution or organisation, and how they are supporting you through the teacher training course.

i) *What is their position on staff continuous professional development (CPD)? Are you supported to improve? How?*
ii) *What are their local expectations on the standards of teachers they'll employ? Do they have a policy for getting new teachers qualified? Do they see a value in this to their quality agenda?*

2. UNDERSTANDING OBSERVATION AS ASSESSMENT

This Chapter will explore the role of the observed teaching practice assessment, both as an assessment tool, and also from the perspective of the trainee teacher; it will introduce aspects for consideration to aid with the preparation for the assessment, as well as some tips to help with making life for the observer-assessor easier, which can only be a good thing for you!

This Chapter relates to the following Professional Standards:

Professional values and attributes *– (1) Evaluate what works best in your teaching and learning to meet the diverse needs of your learners; (2) Evaluate and challenge your practice, values and beliefs; (4) Be creative and innovative in selecting and adapting strategies to help learners to learn*

Professional knowledge and understanding *– (9) Apply theoretical understanding of effective practice in teaching, learning and assessment drawing on research and other evidence; (10) Evaluate your practice with others to assess its impact on learning;*

Professional skills *– (18) Apply appropriate and fair* *methods of assessment and provide constructive and timely feedback to support progression and achievement; (19) Maintain and update your teaching and learning expertise and vocational skills through collaboration with employers; (20) Contribute to organisational development and quality improvement through collaboration with others.*

Observation is often considered to be high ranking in terms of its authenticity as an assessment tool. It allows the assessor to witness first hand the credible actions undertaken by their learners, to make judgments based on the skills and expertise demonstrated "in action" during the period of the test, and provides a meaningful engagement with developmental feedback based on a shared experience.

It is a regular feature of many of the accredited courses within the Learning and Skills sector, especially those that have close affiliations to working practices. Beauty therapists, for example, are observed during their practical assessments, and Teaching Assistants undergo work place observations of their performance. Teaching follows the same model, and rightly so.

Interestingly, observation as an assessment method can provide us with both formative and summative assessment data as an educator, and it is worth taking a couple of moments to ponder on this. As you might expect, in published literature, there has been a mixed bag of reviews about how effective observing teaching can be as an assessment tool.

O'Leary (2014:67) makes the point that learning itself is such a complex and internalised process in the main, that expecting an observer to make substantive judgments on how much new learning has taken place, for example, is questionable.

> **REALITY CHECK:**
>
> *Irrespective of your subject specialism(s), you'll need to be assessing your learners to check on their progress, and identify how well they are attaining new knowledge and acquiring new skills. These observations work in a similar way.*
>
> i) *Reflecting on your own delivery, what range of assessment tools do you use to test learning? How effective are these at actually demonstrating learners' attainment?*
>
> ii) *Do you use observation as an assessment tool? It is often used informally, but consider how you sometimes feel in advance of your own observation – does it impact on your performance? Could the same be happening to your learners? What strategies would you suggest to your learners to combat this – and are you able to apply them to yourself?*

Indeed, O'Leary goes on to point out that even the most experienced observers, who can certainly be relied upon to make informed judgments based on the nuances they identify, cannot do so by merely watching interactions alone; more data is required to support them in this assessment, and only with this can the observation truly be based on sufficient evidence. We'll come back to this in a moment, as using the principles of assessment to discuss how the observation can work for us is a valuable conversation to have. Firstly, however, I'd like to consider how the observation of trainee-teachers fits into the wider picture of formal assessment.

Formal Formative Assessment, or Subjective Summative Assessment?

There's a mouthful. As you will no doubt cover quite early on in your teacher-training course, assessment takes on many faces. There is initial and diagnostic, there is peer- and self-assessment, ipsative assessment rears its head, and we have the extended assessment/learning family: assessment *of* learning, assessment *for* learning, and assessment *as* learning.

Recent thinkers regularly draw parallels between the phase of formative assessment and the use of assessment for learning, with a similar link being made when comparing assessment of learning and the role of summative assessment. It is a fair point, as they are akin to one another in many respects, but how does that help you? Potentially, it could help you quite a lot.

A case could be made that teachers should not be assessed in situ, undertaking the professional role, until they have gained more experience; by experience, I am referring to both the theoretical knowledge accrued by participating in your DET course (or similar), as well as the unquestionable experience gained in your own classroom – in whatever many and varied forms that may take – whilst performing the teacher role.

We wouldn't, after all, think it fair, valid or reasonable to assess one of our own learners too early in a course, would we? Certainly not, yet here we are finding ourselves having to incorporate 4 observations per year (8 if on a fast track programme), all with time in-between to demonstrate our development and growth. Is someone, somewhere, having a laugh?

Actually, it is here that context plays a part. These observations are simultaneously formative and summative, within the teacher-training environment, and that is a good thing. No, really – it is. See, they are formative in so much as they allow your assessor(s) to monitor the progress you make, and provide you with on-going feedback to further support this development.

Similarly, as you complete theoretical components of your course, you will find yourself beginning to take aspects of theory that you've learned, and applying it to your sessions; through the planning, the curriculum design, the way you approach inclusion – whatever it may be, as you complete units, aspects will begin to click together like a never-ending jigsaw, and that is fine. You'll possibly see in your observation reports positive comments against criteria you may previously have struggled with, which is at once both rewarding and affirming.

In the same way, the observations are also an assessment of your learning. The assessors conducting the visits have very clearly defined criteria, which we will dissect over the next few chapters, but nevertheless they do provide a clear structure by which your performance as a teacher can be measured and, in turn, supported. So, whether you feel the observations have a closer affinity with formative or summative assessment, you are still going to be in receipt of developmental feedback that can help you determine how best to continually improve.

Yes – you. The observations do comprise a core element of the assessment strategy for the teacher training programmes, but they are not just there to facilitate a tick-box approach to confer competence upon you. They are formative in the truest sense; every teacher has the responsibility of ensuring they are continuing to perform to the best of their ability, and part of that is to also recognise that perhaps they can do better.

These observations provide you with something that will be significantly less frequent after your course – the critical eyes of someone there to support and encourage you. Of course, quality cycles will no doubt require you to be observed, but that relationship – whilst vital – is likely to be fundamentally different. These observations assess your performance, but they provide you with feedback that should stimulate your creative teacher-mind.

Reflection is an area of intellectual engagement that your course will demand of you regularly. This is sometimes considered a little tedious by some, and self-indulgent navel gazing by others. In all honestly, as with so much in life, what you get out of it tends to depend on what you invest. Every observation you have that assesses your performance provides you with reflective stimuli – some you may contest, much you may have anticipated, but all of it can be used as a springboard for improvement.

Improvement is a watchword for us now and throughout a successful teaching career. Whilst we have seen that the teaching qualifications must demonstrate that trainees cover professional standards, the whole structure is intended to support the trainee in developing their knowledge, skills and teaching practice. Its very mandate is therefore one of improvement. You as the trainee must, of course, play your part and take the reflective stimuli mentioned above and use it to your advantage.

Engaging in professional reflection is a skill you would do well to develop, and let's take a moment now to consider this. Gibbs (1988) is one of many theorists who explore and discuss models of reflection, and as an outcome of every formative observation, applying his reflective cycle (seen in fig 1 below, adapted to lend relevance to your own learning) can prove useful. The six-stage approach presented here allows you to engage with ipsative assessment, drawing on those formative observation findings.

In a later chapter, we'll revisit this further to examine how you can really use your feedback on a longer term scale. For now, however, let's look at what Gibbs was proposing, and how it can relate to your own delivery of teaching, learning and assessment.

Fig 1. Reflective Cycle (after Gibbs, 1988)

Reflective Cycle

Conclusion: *What did you learn? What else could you have done? Assess the impact on you and on your future actions.*

Description: *What happened?*
- *Context*
- *Roles played by you and others*

Text: *How do class readings and lectures relate to your understanding of the incident?*

Feelings: *What were you thinking and feeling at the time? How have those feelings changed?*

Analysis: *What sense can you make of the situation?*
- *Explore details & the 'why' of your judgements.*
- *What challenged you?*

Evaluation: *What was good and bad about the experience? Make a judgement.*

This provides you, as the assessed, the opportunity to make effective use of the observation to both improve your own practice in general, but also to evolve as a practitioner in your own right. Let's briefly consider the stages presented, and how they can add value to your formative assessment observations:

Description: What actually occurred? You can break this down a few ways; for example, you can look at the feedback holistically, and identify any themes or trends that may require attention. You could, instead, tackle the points criterion by criterion. You could even look at the aspects easier to address first, and then move onto those requiring greater thought and adaptation. The beauty is, that the choice is entirely yours.

Feelings: Were you aware at the time that something wasn't going as well as it could? Can you recall any emotive responses – did your instinct tell you to do something else? Did you deviate from the plan when you shouldn't have, or perhaps the reverse is the case?

Evaluation: You've got the observer's professional judgments – do you agree? Can you appreciate why they saw (or think they saw) what they did? Are you aware of anything in addition that went well or otherwise that perhaps the qualification criteria don't cover? Can that influence other aspects of the delivery?

Analysis: If not already, this will become familiar to you as a process, given you'll be doing much analysis on your course. Here, you are applying your analytical processes to what happened in that session. Can you identify why the things that possibly weren't as successful went that way? Alternatively, can you recognise ways to tackle criteria not sufficiently covered in this session, so that they are demonstrable in future observations?

Text: Use your course! You will be, and may already be, engaging with a range of literature on teaching, learning and assessing. This will include planning, delivery, resource use, monitoring progress and structuring your learning programmes.

Can you synthesise solutions/explanations from the literature you have already accessed? Chances are, there will be links to be made between the theory to which you are being exposed, and the practice you are (or aren't yet) adopting. All that wider reading isn't just to help you pad out your assignments (!) – it's also there to help you hone your practice.

Conclusion: So what? No reflection, or focused evaluation of a lesson, is any use unless you apply it. What did you learn from the observation in particular, or the session in general? Can you now see ways (i) to improve on what you did for future sessions, and (ii) should there be any criteria you have not yet covered successfully, can you identify opportunities to ensure your future sessions – especially those you have arranged to be assessed in – where you can effectively display the required skills?

It is to be anticipated that your focus be drawn towards the less positive elements of the report, given these are the priority areas for improvement. It is a wise teacher who also takes ownership of their own strengths – don't lose sight of what you did well, and recognise that progress. Assessment, even for trainee teachers, isn't just about the negative.

REALITY CHECK:

Consider the last session you delivered, and make two lists – one of what went well, and one of what you wish had gone better.

Congratulate yourself for the first list, but now practise using the reflective cycle above to tackle the second list – can you take pre-emptive measures before your next observation based on these findings? Ipsative assessment (in simple terms) can be used as a structured form of self-assessment that can be very useful, allowing you to measure your own progress – can you see your progress reflecting on these same lists after your next session?

Assessment in Principle: Validating Observed Teaching Practice

All assessments should conform to clear principles, and the observation of teaching and learning within the context of a teacher training qualification is no exception. Whilst both the assessor and the assessed have their own responsibilities in the assessment process, it is important to remember the principles that underpin effective assessment so that you, in your role as the assessed, can have confidence in the activity of being observed, but more, that you can do your bit to support the smooth running of the visit.

Gravells (2011, 18) reminds us of the VASCR approach, which we'll be looking at next. It is worth directing you at this point to the vast contribution made by Gravells to the literature that supports trainee teachers – her work spans all of the key areas of study, and is very accessible. Well worth a read, if you can. For the here and the now, let's talk principles as they relate to our topic.

Validity – *the assessment instrument is appropriate and is measuring (or testing) that which should be tested. From the perspective of assessing your teaching practice, then it is a clearly defined tool. The criteria are linked to the professional standards of the sector, and are readily available. The assessors are aware of what they are looking for, and will usually be experienced observers across a range of specialist subjects. This last point is important – on a very rare number of occasions, one or two trainee teachers have spoken to me with concerns that their observer was not watching them the whole time. Indeed, they were very, very concerned that the assessor was more interested in filling in their observation form than watching the session. Let's put this one to bed – observers don't just observe with their eyes.*

Experienced observers are usually very well aware of what is going on around them without looking at every single moment. So much can be gleaned from listening to an exchange between the teacher and the learners, or between learners themselves, that you may be taken aback. The detail, quality and tone of verbal feedback; the way learners interpret instructions; the pace and structure of the session; the use of resources and the way the teacher communicates – this and more can all be absorbed by attentive listening and subtle looking. As observers, we do try to be unobtrusive (believe it or not) and by not staring wildly into the class, learners are usually put at ease much quicker, as the observer seems less significant. So yes, I'll accept we might not be watching, but we never stop observing – don't you ever worry about that!

Authenticity – *This relates directly to the work being assessed, which in this case is your teaching, and the associated aspects. In many ways, as mentioned earlier, observation is one of the best assessment methods for ensuring authenticity, because the assessor is a live witness that the work being presented/undertaken is that of the candidate. The same applies here, of course, but some might argue that rather than it being a genuine snapshot of your teaching, it is an opportunity to grandstand the criteria; to impress within a somewhat artificial bubble that is divorced from the normal delivery that your learners receive.*

In most cases, this is an unfounded argument; your naturally occurring documentation, for example, such as session plans, a scheme of work, assessment records all clearly demonstrate to an experienced observer that your practice is consistent and not put in place for a one-off event. You can also do much to support that, and I'll come back to this later. However, in a minority of cases, there may be a degree of truth to this, but not without good reason. In several years of delivering teacher-training programmes, it has become very clear that one size does not naturally fit all.

Trainee teachers working in private training providers, or in charity organisations, for example, sit outside of the more traditionally recognised standards that these qualifications represent. To meet mandatory aspects of these nationally defined standards, some teachers have had to adopt practices that – whilst may have positive impacts upon their planning and assessing, and ultimately their delivery – are actions that perhaps are not routinely demanded within their normal working conditions. This can be a bone of contention for these teachers, but the course is the course is the course; if they or their employer wishes them to hold a full level 4 or level 5 qualification as a teacher, then this cannot simply be handed over. Skills need to be demonstrated, and yes – in some corners of the sector, they may be skills used less frequently. Does that make them less valuable skills to have? Arguably not, and again in my experience, once moving passed the initial resistance, the vast majority of teachers sitting in this category find that the broadening of their horizons has been to the benefit of their teaching, and not the detriment. Nothing worth achieving is always easy to attain, after all.

Currency – This links to the relevance of the work and the assessment. Certainly, from the formal assessment aspect, the current standards will be underpinning the performance criteria that the assessors will be using, but how well are you demonstrating current practices? This is an important aspect to the delivery and the planning – you are being assessed on what you are delivering, so make sure it is current in its own right. There may be nothing wrong with recycled lesson plans, but they are only valuable if they have been tweaked to reflect the current learners, and any associated considerations. More on this will be raised in the next chapter on planning for the observations, but it is common sense – make sure the dates reflect the session being observed, and not one from two years ago! Unlikely? You'd be surprised...

Sufficiency – The observed aspects of the qualification are intended to be revisited over the duration of the course, so in most cases a minimum of 8 times. Operating much as Bruner's *'spiral curriculum' model proposes (1960), this allows you to experience and build upon key aspects of the essential skills you need to demonstrate – and develop – over time. Never heard of the 'spiral curriculum'? Don't worry, it's an easy one to research, and could very well come in handy on your course (spoilers!). The frequency of the visits should allow you time to incorporate feedback from previous observations (possibly having applied Gibb's reflective cycle (1988) to support you in your preparation), and ensure that you are providing sufficient evidence to allow the observer to make the necessary judgements. If nothing else, this shows you already applying a theory to your practice!*

The process of the assessed teaching and learning observation requires a range of product evidence to be available to support your overall performance, and this should reflect on-going use, rather than stand-alone, one-off approaches as far as is possible. To aid the observer in having confidence in your professional practice, bear this in mind when preparing for their visit. Make their life easier so that in turn, yours can be easier too. The more you pre-empt what they need to see and supply it, the less work you'll need to do to play catch-up in future observations.

Reliability – *This principle expects that criteria are applied in the same fashion at all assessed visits, and for all individual learners. Additionally, it presupposes that all those conducting the assessment do so applying the same approach to, and appreciation of, the standards in question. An important point to note here is that, in some institutions, those undertaking the assessed visits may also have a role in the quality assurance work of the college (or similar). Where this is the case, their appreciation of the standards could, understandably, become entwined with other classroom observational frameworks. As such, it is not impossible that these influences can creep into the report writing. In most cases, this may add value to the depth of the feedback you receive, but from your own perspective, it may* *be worth ensuring that the criteria remain the focus of the report, rather than other aspects that – whilst relevant to the quality infrastructure of the organisation – may not best support your achievement of the qualification. As with any formal assessment, it may be prudent to be aware of how to appeal a decision, in the unlikely event you have concerns.*

REALITY CHECK:

There's much written about the different principles of assessment, types of assessment, and indeed the range of assessment methods available to educators.

i) *There are a lot of terms within 'education-speak' that may mean one thing to us, and something entirely different to people in the outside world; for example, most people would see 'assessment' and 'evaluation' as the same thing, but we know differently. Keeping track of this can be tricky, especially for new recruits to the profession, so don't worry if you need to revise what different terms mean*

ii) *Consider setting up an educational glossary, into which you can add terms as you come across them – then you have your own easy access reference book. Why not start with 'Assessment' and cover the types, phases and principles? It can only come in handy – plus creating it may well help you remember!*

The Coexistence of Assessment and Learning: making it work for you

This chapter has served to illustrate the role of the observation as an assessment tool; an instrument to be used to both support your development and progress, and provide demonstrable evidence of your skills and learning. Much can be achieved through the use of observation in this way and, as mentioned in the previous chapter, only truly in the arena of teaching itself can you authentically show the application of your learning as a trainee teacher, far more than even your well-executed written assignments.

The observation serves as an opportunity to apply assessment for learning, as through engagement with the process, learning itself should take place. You will recognise ways and means to improve, and the overview provided by your assessor can lend itself greatly to extending your scope to improve. You must, of course, engage fully with this process to reap any benefit. Indeed, over time (and this will vary from individual to individual) you will be far more confident with your delivery during these assessed visits, and this will make the observer's task much easier. The confidence of a teacher thriving in a classroom makes the completion of such an observation much more straightforward for both parties.

So, it is clear to see the central role of these teaching practice assessments to the overall strategy of any teacher training course, and in common with any test you can take steps to prepare for it. Whilst in the upcoming chapters we will be considering some specifics around the performance criteria, let's take a moment or two now to reflect on ways we can begin to get ourselves in the right frame of mind for these visits.

Firstly, panic. No, that's not a suggestion, rather something to avoid. Panic is usually generated in this context by a sense of anxiety around being under-prepared, and watched.

This is something you have complete control over, and should maximise to the fullest extent. You should be able to negotiate when you are going to be observed (within reason), so no formally assessed visit would ever be unannounced. For one thing, that would be a significant breach of the principles of assessment. This already gives you the opportunity to lay the groundwork for the session and be ready. In common with any practical exam, you know what is expected of you – so make sure you bring it to the proverbial table.

Leave yourself time. Always a premium in any branch of education and training, time is so valuable. Arrive for your session in advance so you can set things up – this should allow you the space to not have to rush, as this is where small errors can creep in that rise up to bite you later.

Pace yourself, and if you've done it well, you can afford a few moments to chat to your assessor when they arrive to give them the context of the session, as well as draw their attention to anything you feel may be relevant. For example, you may have had to make an adaptation to one of your planned activities to accommodate one of your learners, who has very specific requirements. This is a useful conversation to have.

Avoid conversations that are unhelpful – don't waffle at your assessor; this betrays a degree of under-confidence, and you don't want to let yourself fall into that trap. Believe in what you have planned, and keep extraneous chatter to a minimum if you know it is something that makes your nerves surface. A good assessor knows you'll be a little nervous, because they know you care and want to do well. Niceties are useful, but stay in control.

Identify in advance where you want them to sit – but ensure it is somewhere that grants them sight of you, your learners, and allows them to look at any documents or folders you wish them to see without encroaching too much on the class itself. This shows you as a well-organised and together teacher. It also sets you up to perform well – a positive pre-class leads into a successful session. Remember to introduce your assessor to the class. Observations are pretty routine these days, so learners are increasingly used to having someone pop in to watch proceedings.

It can be more distracting to have a stranger in the corner and have no-one say anything about them. You don't have to say they are your assessor, if you feel it might diminish your authority with your group, but at least let them know the name of the observer, even if you just roll out the clichéd *"they're here to watch me, not you"* line so often used (albeit inaccurately) to reassure learners. Remember, your assessor is looking to see how you make the teaching and learning environment safe for the learners to participate in; they are less likely to participate, with a silent stranger taking notes. *Break that ice – everyone will feel better for it!*

In the next chapter we'll reflect more on the impact of your planning, with specific focus on the criteria that links to this. We can also build upon the themes in this chapter, and look at some advance planning you can do to make sure those observations really show you and your practice in the best light possible.

REALITY CHECK:

Consider the session you are next going to be observed delivering. Think about the layout – where can you put the assessor so they can do all they need to without disrupting your learners?

- *What does the assessor need to see during your assessment visit to help them confirm how you're meeting the standards? Can you provide it easily?*
- *What information can you provide the assessor verbally, when they arrive, to make the observation run as smoothly as possible? Is there anything about individual learners that they need to know? Anything about the structure of the session that may not be immediately clear on the session plan?*
- *Make yourself a checklist – preparation is the key!*

3 PLANNING, PLANNING, PLANNING!

This chapter will explore the role of the advanced planning with regards to your formal teaching practice assessment, in terms of the criteria to be demonstrated that surrounds your planning for the session, your learners and so forth, but also any planning you need to consider to make the assessed observation as smooth as possible.

This chapter relates to the following Professional Standards:

Professional values and attributes – *(1) Evaluate what works best in your teaching and learning to meet the diverse needs of your learners; (2) Evaluate and challenge your practice, values and beliefs; (4) Be creative and innovative in selecting and adapting strategies to help learners to learn; (5) Value and promote social and cultural diversity, equality of opportunity and inclusion*

Professional knowledge and understanding – *(9) Apply theoretical understanding of effective practice in teaching, learning and assessment drawing on research and other evidence; (10) Evaluate your practice with others to assess its impact on learning; (11); Manage and* *promote positive learner behaviour; (12) Understand the teaching and professional role and your responsibilities*

Professional skills – *(14) Plan and deliver effective learning programmes for diverse groups; (16) Address the mathematics and English needs of learners, and work creatively to overcome individual barriers to learning; (17) Enable learners to share responsibility for their own learning and assessment, setting goals that stretch and challenge; (18) Apply appropriate and fair methods of assessment and provide constructive and timely feedback to support progression and achievement*

There's an old adage: 'fail to prepare, prepare to fail' and for teachers this is most certainly true; for trainee teachers, perhaps even more so. So much of the success or otherwise of a lesson is directly linked to the quality and depth of planning put in before hand.

On this, it is prudent to make one thing absolutely clear from the start – planning takes time. For some, it takes very little time; natural planners work swiftly and find their lessons come together with ease. Others, arguably the majority, take quite some time cogitating over how to plan for their ideal sessions. Simply put, there is no 'one true way' to plan. One of my DET learners, a keep-fit teacher working in ACL, told me of the most challenging aspect of the observation for her:

"...the hardest thing I find is the lesson plan. It's making sure I cover all the aspects expected, and articulate it on paper."

This is not uncommon, and we'll hear more from learners and their views on planning for observations shortly.

It is worth mentioning that lesson plan formats vary significantly from organisation to organisation; some are quite loosely structured, others are more demanding of content. Whatever your organisation uses, remember this – it's simply a tool, it's what you do with it that counts.

Genuinely, any blank lesson plan has the potential to be the blueprint for either an outstanding lesson, or a disastrous one. Whilst other factors could, arguably, influence this, there is only one real determining element – you. You alone have the power to complete the lesson plan, to make sure that within it you demonstrate how you are taking into consideration all of the essential components of your class, and this chapter will explore this in much more detail.

Before we move onto that, however, and indeed start examining the mandatory criteria for the observed assessment that links to planning, I'd like you to consider this. A lesson plan is not really where you plan your session, it is simply where you record that planning. The actual process takes place as a concept in your mind – ideas coalescing, merging and evolving. Perhaps you convert these into a PowerPoint (or similar) presentation first, or perhaps you create some engaging resources as a centrepiece of an activity – perhaps you sit quietly staring at the computer screen as you visualise your lesson in your mind's eye first. Whatever your particular process, the lesson plan itself is merely the repository for the product of that process.

Important to remember, and often forgotten, is that whilst the lesson plan is indeed a tool for you to use, it is also an auditable document. It serves many masters other than just the teacher who created it; your organisation's quality management, for example, external regulators (such as Ofsted), and as a way of charting your development on teacher training programmes. No wonder, then, given its significance, that so many people find it a challenge.

Creating Inclusive Teaching & Learning Plans

The formal observation consists of a range of performance evidence that must be demonstrated across the in-situ assessed lessons. The majority of this is performance evidence in the most literal sense – you need to be seen *doing*. However, embedded within the performance evidence are some criteria that are mostly confirmed by your assessor through a combination of what actually takes place, and how closely this aligns to what you planned for.

This chapter will explore those planning related criteria, and examine how you might ensure you demonstrate your competency. Remember, developing a lesson that meets the needs of individual learners, as well as stretching and challenging them all appropriately, is a key responsibility of the professional teacher. A scribbled list of what you want to cover is by no means likely to measure up. Outstanding sessions do not happen by accident – they take time to plan; it is an outstanding teacher who makes it look spontaneous and effortless but, believe me, the effort has most definitely been applied.

Let us consider the following criteria:

- *Confirm how the candidate has designed teaching and learning plans which respond to: (i) the individual goals and needs of learners; and (ii) curriculum requirements*
- *Confirm how the candidate has used inclusive teaching and learning approaches, including technologies, to meet the individual needs of learners*

Both of these criteria require you to take individual needs into consideration – and the lesson plan is a terrific way to record your planning for this. Historically, trainee-teachers (and some more experienced teachers too, alas), felt it best practice to make overt adaptations to their planning to almost single out where they had taken steps to be 'inclusive.' The irony, of course, is that by being so overt, the individuals in question were far from included at all.

The real skill with inclusive teaching and learning approaches is that the very nature of the inclusivity should really be seamless; invisible to the naked eye, almost. This is not easy, and is something that will develop over time. But it is here that the lesson plan can be so very useful – it is here that the lesson plan allows you to demonstrate the quality of your planning. But we'll come back to that in a moment.

First let's reflect on how a lesson plan responds to individual goals. The short answer is that it can't, not in isolation. As the teacher, you need to have established your learners' individual goals. Let's take a moment to consider how and why you do this through a few frequently asked questions...

Why do I need to establish individual goals – surely their goal is to complete my course? So whilst of course your learners' overall goal is to complete and achieve on your course, they are going to have some personal aims, or milestones if you like, that they can hit along the way. Additionally, whether you are delivering a qualification course or not, identifying these milestones can help you demonstrate your flexibility and creativity as a teacher in taking steps to ensure your content links to these milestones, and in turn, makes your learners' experience more personalised and so even better.

Recording individual goals sounds a lot like more paperwork – what difference does it actually make? This question has two answers. Firstly, and arguably the more critical, is that it helps you to do your job. Too often I have heard trainees tell me that their organisation doesn't require learners to have individual goals set, so why should they bother? This is a very frustrating question to anyone who takes the teaching profession seriously! As a professional teacher, it is your personal responsibility to make sure that what you are delivering is meeting individual needs and interests, therefore it is your responsibility to capture these and – significantly – use them to inform your planning. This can be your overall scheme of work, when plotting or revising your content, or at session plan level. Either way, this supports you in being better equipped to support your learners.

The second answer to this question is a little less exciting to a teacher, but nevertheless important. As you'll have noticed from reading Chapter One, education is a political football, and whilst it may not always attract much funding, it does attract scrutiny. Much like a business that requires auditors, education has its regulators, such as Ofsted, who need to see that organisations touched by public money (so FE colleges, private training providers with a Skills Funding Agency contract, etc.) are delivering their product in a 'value for money' way. To achieve this, inspectors (and worthwhile internal quality management processes) need to be able to audit that learning is taking place. As a teacher working in this industry, it is part of your role to contribute to your organisation's quality assurance processes, and part of that is the production of clear evidence that learning is taking place. Setting and tracking the achievement of individual goals are key parts of that process. We will look at tracking progress a little later, in Chapter Four – but in order to do this effectively, you need to establish some of these milestones. Yes, some will naturally occur due to the course itself, but finding out what your learners want (or need) to learn contributes to this. If you are worrying about paperwork, then teaching may not be the best route for you.

But how do I find out what these personal goals are? It sounds like a lot of extra work on top of what I'm expected to do. To put the record straight, it isn't 'on top' of what is already expected of a teacher, it is a core part of the teacher's role. The fact not every organisation sets this as a requirement is a reflection on them, not the professional teacher who will want this information to do the best job they can. Now we've cleared that up, let's look at the real issue here – how.

There are many ways, and yes, some will take more time than others. Some teachers have the luxury of a pre-course interview with their potential learners, and identifying some of these goals can easily be a part of this interview process. Asking questions like *'what are the particular aspects of the course that you really want to explore, and why?'* can help focus them on their own goals and so inform you. Similarly, asking *'what are your ultimate goals following on from this course?'* will give you a sense of why they want to do the course, which may allow you to identify areas of the subject that will be of particularly value to them – after all, they may not know what they need to know to achieve their personal goals, but as the professional in this equation, you might.

Often, a formal pre-course interview is not possible for every course, but this doesn't stop you asking the same kind of questions. Some teachers have incorporated this sort of activity into early icebreakers, and recorded the information themselves. Others have provided short questionnaire-type tasks as part of the initial assessment process, to maximise time, so that all learners can provide the information in a compressed amount of time. This requires you to review these after the event, and record them appropriately, but at least you have the information.

This covers goals, but what do we mean by the term 'needs' in this context? Most commonly, this applies to any specific learning needs that should be addressed to ensure inclusivity. For example, are any of your learners dyslexic? Perhaps they suffer from chronic fatigue syndrome? Does your session fall during a period of fasting for some religions? These are all features of individual needs that could legitimately manifest in your classes. Are you, however, taking them into consideration? Does your learning plan/session plan/lesson plan (call it what you will) reflect this?

In short, you want the answer here to be a resounding yes.

Before, I mentioned that education, and learning itself, both need to be auditable. As a teacher you produce key evidence to contribute to that audit, including assessment records, and centrally, your session plans. It is in the plan for your lesson that you can clearly show how you have taken into consideration any individual goals and planned to make links to these. This does not mean that every lesson you are recording a way of supporting every goal – that's highly unlikely to be possible. But you may well have one or two aspects of what you'll be covering in any given session that relate directly to one or more of your learners' individual goals. On your plan, you can make direct reference to this.

Your plan may have a section dedicated to recognising where you are linking to your learners' goals. Failing that, you may find it most appropriate to record the links within the body of the plan, as part of your differentiation. Within the FE and ACL sector, a range of different session plan formats is available, and it would take a separate book to explore what works well, and how best to structure your planning.

However, remember that whatever format you use, it needs to be a tool that is fit for purpose. It has to work for you, and enable you to effectively structure your intended activities, and show how you take into consideration these individual goals, as well as any individual needs. Whilst a far more shallow consideration, an effectively completed session plan that shows how you have planned to meet the needs/support the goals of Learners X and Y makes the observer's job of confirming your competence that little bit easier.

So what does this look like, you ask? It can vary, of course, and sadly for all of us there is no single, model way of recording this. That said, there are some better ways of approaching it, and that isn't always the model provided by the Awarding Institution for your qualification.

Let us consider the types of headings you may recognise in your session plan, or indeed that you may wish to include in your session plan if they are presently absent. The latter may require discussion with your line manager for permission, but it may well be a conversation worth having. Headings, whether for columns or sections, are important because they remind and direct you towards the aspects that, as a professional teacher, you really want (by which I really mean need) to include.

Below, I'll talk you through a series of headings that I would expect to see in a lesson plan. I make no suggestion about structure or layout – that's not overly important here, as long as it is readable – my focus is solely on the areas you will want a lesson plan to cover for it to demonstrate that it is inclusive, and meets individual needs.

Building Your Inclusive Teaching & Learning Plans

As mentioned, there is no 'one true way' to present a lesson plan (in the same way people refer to them as session plans, lesson plans, learning plans and so on; I'll deliberately use as many names as possible as wherever you work you'll need to acclimatise to the terms they use). But ultimately it is content that counts, both for your qualification but also for you to perform your job effectively and professionally. Below is the list of headings you'd benefit from incorporating into your learning plans, and a brief description of what one might expect to be covered:

AIMS – *that which the teacher is expecting to cover, and in many ways are the key topic(s) and drive of the session.*

OBJECTIVES/OUTCOMES – *that which the learners are expected to achieve within the planned session. These should be as specific as possible to avoid ambiguity and to allow the teacher (you) to assess learners against the achievement of these.*

Objectives can also be constructed to support the achieving of individual learner goals in certain sessions where this is viable. You can also differentiate objectives based on the levels within your group, thus still challenging and stretching individuals within their range of ability. Please don't ever use 'understand' as the opening to an objective! It is hard to assess understanding – opt instead for something like 'demonstrate' or 'explain' or 'identify' etc, as these are all things you can quantify. More on this in the next chapter!

SUPPORT FOR LEARNERS – *if you have any Learning Support Assistants (LSA), it is wise to record that support, and what it is you need them to do within the session. LSAs are there to ensure inclusivity, but often need direction from the teacher to be fully effective. How you plan to use them is an indicator of your planning. Additionally, you may need specific resources to support the learning of individuals – it is useful to record this here, and share a copy with the LSA for clarity.*

LINKS TO LEARNERS' GOALS – *a valuable section that can explicitly identify that you have captured learners' goals, and how those specific goals will be covered/contributed to/achieved within the planned session.*

SUBJECT MATTER/TOPIC – *clarity about what is being specifically examined and explored at any given point. This is also supported by the inclusion of effective timings within the session – how you break down the ways you communicate the topic(s), or the elements of the topic, into manageable segments to allow for learners to assimilate the information and engage with it meaningfully. Too often, trainee teachers assign 40 minutes (or similar) to cover a topic, not realising that they are actually undertaking several activities etc. in that time, that if broken down more succinctly, would allow them to much more effectively plan for differentiation, and allow observers to see the extent of their planning more clearly.*

TEACHER ACTIVITY – *this should clearly outline what the teacher (still you) is doing at any given point in the session. This can range from introducing and presenting the topic, to chairing an in-class debate, to monitoring the progress of group work. It should remain specific throughout.*

LEARNER ACTIVITY – *similarly to the teacher activity, the planned learner activity should be clear, and broken down for each stage of the session. It could be that they are listening and taking notes, or it could be that they are participating in a group presentation, or even undertaking in-class online investigation into a particular aspect of the topic. Again, this needs to be explicit, so grouping too much activity together makes this harder to time-manage; break it down and your session time management is easier to adhere to (as well as allow observers to monitor).*

DIFFERENTIATION – *a section or column that provides a degree of detail around how you have planned to differentiate within the session, and for whom (in some cases).*

This can also link back to your differentiated learning outcomes, as well as the achievement of, or specific focus on, individual goals for certain learners.

EQUALITY & DIVERSITY – *a much underexploited aspect of planning. Promoting equality in a session should always be a priority; if you have had to make any adaptations to resources or to your activities, then please include this here. Remember this should be seamless and, as far as is possible it should not draw attention to any individual learners. It may also be prudent to include here the assigned duties of an LSA if you have one in the session, as this will make it clear to both them and any observer what you are expecting them to do at any given point either within the class overall or with designated learners. The celebration of diversity, the recognition of the differences that enrich our cultures and experiences, as well as wider cultural awareness, should always be present as added value to the subject matter, not something shoehorned into a session to tick a box.*

Good observers, much like inspectors, will not be impressed with references being made for the sake of it – any wider references to the world at large, and other communities, should be naturally occurring and enhance the learning experience rather than dilute it. Learners are not attending to have the history of Valentine's Day explained to them, just because your session falls the same week. However, if you are delivering something whereby perhaps this can be a source of influence (such as floristry, or card making, or hospitality) then there may be mileage in exploring the impact of such a date, and setting the short research task for your learners to identify equivalent or broadly similar days of celebration within other cultures, that could also be influencers on their work. This can require some additional research, but in augmenting the effectiveness and quality of your sessions, it can most certainly be worth it. Just remember – it needs to be organically linked to your lesson, not something bolted on for effect.

*PROMOTION OF ENGLISH & MATHS – this is something we will look at a little more in the next section focusing on curriculum requirements, but nevertheless, it is something that needs to be a feature of modern session plans. The promotion and development of learners' English and mathematics skills is central to the Government's FE agenda at the time of writing that translates into all our practice. Again, this is not something that necessarily features in every aspect of every moment of your session, but you need to be conscious of your responsibility to advance this agenda. Whether you are getting learners to work out percentages within the natural flow of the topic, or you are challenging their grammar and/or spelling to ensure it is correct (and they appreciate **why** it is correct), or expanding their vocabulary through discussions about word origins or common roots when introducing new terminology, you must ensure you are actively engaged in this aspect of the role. This may require you to brush up your own English and maths skills too!*

ASSESSMENT – *whether this is assessment of learning, assessment for learning, or assessment as learning, you need to incorporate clearly what your particular assessment strategies for each session are. This can be a mix of formal and informal methods; for example, group discussions or presentations can act as assessment methods just as well as questions and answers, quizzes and test papers.*

Something else we will be looking at further in Chapter Four is the use of peer and self-assessment methods. These are often overlooked, but form a key part of the classroom observation criteria for trainee teachers; you need to make use of these approaches, and plan for them. There are many creative ways to deploy them, and whilst there are of course potential pitfalls, when used well, they can be valuable to learners and teacher alike.

> ***REALITY CHECK:***
>
> ***Take a look at the lesson plan format you use in your current work setting, and compare it to the list above.***
>
> ***Whilst the terms may be different, how closely do the headings align? Do you use them effectively to make it clear what is happening with all participants at any given point?***
>
> ***Could someone unfamiliar with your subject walk in and follow what was happening? Could someone familiar with your subject use your plan to teach your lesson?***

It goes without saying that a cursory review of that list implies that this planning malarkey is much more complex than many initially think. It doesn't help that those suggested requirements are presented as a list – makes it look pretty hefty, I know. But worry not, because when presented in a session plan format, these things become inter-related and much more logical to complete than they may initially appear here.

It has been mentioned a few times thus far, but it remains a point worth repeating – planning well takes time. How much varies from teacher to teacher, but so too does the quality of said planning. Don't listen to people who tell you it only takes them half an hour to plan – remember you have no idea how flimsy their planning may be, nor do you know whether their sessions are any good!

So, don't try to measure yourself against others when it comes to planning – everyone approaches it their own way and everyone takes their own time. You will learn much from your planning, yes when it goes resoundingly well, but also when it goes spectacularly badly. And it will – it does at some point for everyone go spectacularly badly (even if you have planned to the nth degree), because there will be that unexpected element you just didn't take into consideration. But on the plus side? It'll never be unexpected again!

Responding to Curriculum Requirements

Reflecting back on the required criteria, you need to demonstrate how you ensure your planning takes curriculum requirements into consideration. Before you can do this, of course, you need to be quite clear on how best to interpret the term' curriculum requirements.' Firstly, there are nationally and locally determined curriculum requirements for you to consider. Let's break these down:

Nationally determined curriculum requirements: This can subdivide further between national standards and national expectations. In terms of the national standards, this relates explicitly to the demands established by the syllabus of your course. Needless to say, this aspect is really only pertinent should you be delivering a certificated qualification course. The criteria of any such programme are usually ratified at a national level, resulting in formal qualification approval by the Office of Qualifications and Examinations Regulation (Ofqual). These requirements can easily be demonstrated through the inclusion of said criteria within the aims of the session, or indeed within the learning objectives.

Some experienced teachers like to include reference to specific criteria being covered within the body of the session plan as well as the overall scheme of work. This is a particularly useful approach to adopt, as it allows you to keep a clear track of the required, indicative content of the qualification course as well as auditable evidence that you have delivered on what is expected. In addition, it also enables you to be particularly precise when it comes to what you are assessing at various points within the session.

It is always useful, whether it is a qualification course or not, to ensure that the observer can have sight of your scheme of work, as mentioned above; this serves to demonstrate your wider planning skills (and that your individual session fits well into a considered, sequential delivery plan). It also serves to further identify your planned assessment strategy, which we will talk more about in the next chapter, but it is something that needs to be seen to have been considered – and implemented – within your observed session.

Aside from formally determined, national curriculum requirements, there are also those that are expected to be in place. These are not, perhaps, evidently explicit in any qualification syllabus, but that isn't surprising; these requirements apply to anyone delivering any type of course under the umbrella of public funding. It is the role of Ofsted, and, on occasion, auditors from the funding agencies, to ensure that these curriculum requirements are being met.

These requirements are often a slightly moveable feast, which isn't overly helpful here, but a committed and professional teacher will pick up on these; usually your institution will require their teachers to incorporate A, B or C into the sessions, or have documentation that details how the teacher tracks and records X and Y, for example. This is reflective of current trends within education, and many teachers make the mistake of thinking their managers are trying to make more work for them! In the case of good managers, quite the reverse is true.

By setting out these requirements, your institution is making sure that you are effectively supporting the governmental view of education's role, and that you will have everything you need in place to make your life (and, in fairness, your employer's life) easier when inspectors call. Of course, institutions vary, and so too do managers, but I'll leave it to you to make the judgement on your own setting. What is important, and should not be lost sight of, is that you – as the professional teacher – assume responsibility as part of your role for delivering on what the government's 'agenda du jour' may be. It is your responsibility to keep up to date with what is expected in your sector, and to implement it. Don't necessarily depend on the generosity of others to keep you informed.

There are, however, some easy and quick wins. For example, at the time of writing, the promotion and development of English and mathematics (EM) skills in all learners is a key government priority. Good lesson plans demonstrate how this is being implemented within any given session, and your lesson plan should be no different.

This is, not to say that every single element of your planned session needs to be advancing learners' EM, but it does mean that you need to take this into consideration. Your own teacher on your teacher-training course should cover this for you quite early on, when exploring the differences between developing the EM skills of your learners, and evidencing your own minimum core skills. Often, inexperienced teachers believe these to be the same. They are not!

To clarify, the minimum core emerged as a requirement for teachers as part of the 2007 reforms discussed in Chapter One (I told you history would be useful). It originally covered the teacher's English (literacy, communication and so forth) skills, their maths skills, and their computing (ICT) skills. The established standard was that all teachers should be demonstrably confident up to, and including, Level 2 in all three areas. However, it was not sufficient to hold Level 2 qualifications in these areas; the teacher must be able to support their learners' individual skills gaps to the required level. For this to be possible, the teacher (and yes, I'm talking about you here) needs to have the confidence to apply those skills.

As a teacher, you can demonstrate your minimum core skills in many ways, and there are other textbooks available that can support you in this in more depth. From our perspective here, though, the lesson plan is somewhere you can evidence both your own minimum core skills and how you are supporting EM skills in your learners with relative ease. It comes down to your own awareness of how and when you are applying these skills, as well as anticipating how and when you can promote and develop your learners' EM skills.

Consider for a moment the next session you are planning to deliver. Look at the topics you are planning to cover, and the activities you are looking to use in order to communicate said topics. Are you introducing any new terminology? If so, can you explain – or see if the learners can explain – the origin or source of the new terminology? That is getting them to either use their English skills, or extend them if they don't initially know. Expanding learners' vocabulary is a perfectly acceptable way of developing their English skills.

If you teach a modern foreign language, you may think developing English skills is less likely to be a feature of your sessions. Having trained well over 50 modern foreign language (MFL) teachers, one thing is abundantly clear – learners all too frequent absence of sufficient English grammar knowledge to fully support the acquisition of the second or other language. Many MFL teachers find much of their earlier sessions (as well as many later ones) are concerned with retreading English grammar so that their learners are suitably equipped to grapple with the grammatical requirements of the course. So, no matter the subject, there will be scope to develop English skills.

Mathematical skills can also be incorporated, even if it is something as fundamental as making learners responsible for their own time management during activities; you set them a task to complete in 10 minutes, for example, and ensure they divide the time/chores up appropriately to maximize the use of their peers and meet the deadline. Any activity requiring the use of measurements (including weights, distance, time, temperature, ingredients) promotes the use of maths skills. Similarly, any problem-solving tasks you might set will usually require some form of numeric reasoning to reach a solution.

In terms of evidencing your own minimum core, it is often more readily proven in its lack of obviousness. For example, a session plan, handouts, scheme of work, presentation that contains no errors of grammar or spelling is a demonstration of your English skills (possibly also your IT skills if you have produced everything well, via a computer). However, where grammar or spelling errors are evident, this is a glaring gap in your minimum core.

In much the same way, numeracy skills gaps can be highlighted if your timings are so loose (or completely inaccurate) as to demonstrate to an observer that you can't estimate the time required for activities to be completed. Similarly, incomplete numbers of resources (when it is within your control) also suggests poor planning and, frankly, counting. I'll be ending the chapter later with a list of bug-bears and tips for success, but here is an advance spoiler – timings overall. You'd be amazed at how often trainee-teachers don't check the timings on their session plans actually add up to the duration of the session. This is both a minimum core and an overall planning issue – as either you have planned too much for your lesson, or not enough, and worse – hadn't noticed! Always make sure the timings on the session add up to the length of the session. It really isn't too difficult!

Locally determined curriculum requirements: This sub-division is arguably easier to manage. Whilst every institution will have its own foibles regarding what documentation needs to be used, how, and in what way, this is usually linked to the external demands of regulators, covered above. Rather than re-tread that ground, let's look at it from the perspective of your delivery, if you are delivering a non-qualification course.

Already, the absence of a qualification means you have no formal, nationally ratified syllabus to use, which in turn affords you quite the degree of freedom to plan you course to genuinely meet the needs of your learners. Whereas those delivering a qualification course may struggle initially to find obvious ways to link their content to specific individual goals, given the pressures of delivery time and so forth, those without the complications of external assessment requirements and pre-determined criteria have somewhat more flexibility in the structuring of their course to meet such needs and interests of their learners.

But you're not off the hook; you still need a curriculum to deliver. You'll still need to assess your learners against something – and excitingly, this is where you have a lot of creative input. You are the creator and designer of your course, so you know what needs to be included, and when (to best allow learners to engage with topics in a learnable sequence and pace). In addition, you will also then be able to establish your own core criteria for the subject, based on what it is you know you need to cover. In essence, you create your own syllabus. This can take the shape of your scheme of work, as a document that can translate your curriculum into a workable blueprint for delivery. Fortuitously, if you don't have formal curriculum requirements to meet, you can have your own, and the scheme of work will help evidence this, not least as it will demonstrate where your observed session fits into the bigger picture.

As an added bonus, you'll also, very early in the course, have identified those all important individual goals we spoke about earlier in this chapter – here you can really use them to both the learners' and your own advantage by demonstrating your flexibility though incorporating these goals into suitable points on your course. You can then also incorporate these targets into the individualised criteria you have developed for your course. These can then be recorded on an assessment tracking sheet, your scheme of work and – when applicable to the lesson in question – your session plan.

It should go without saying, but it is worth ensuring you book your observed visits to sessions where you know you'll be demonstrating this, so that your observer can see it in action, and confirm you are meeting the criteria.

Don't panic about creating your own criteria – this may well be the first time you've ever had to do this, so here are a few suggestions on how to approach it:

1. Borrow from established practice. By this I mean look to any formally accredited courses that are similar to your own, except that they are externally certificated. You can see how it is structured, and you'll see the required

learning outcomes, and how they are worded. You may be able to adapt some of these to suit your own course.

2. Consider what you need to include. If it is an essential aspect of the subject you're delivering, then chances are it's something you need to see your learners have absorbed; convert it into a criteria.

3. Think about wording. Be precise in the criteria – don't make it too woolly or vague; equally, make it clear how you expect it to be evidenced. For example, a criterion that reads *identify and list all the primary and secondary colours* is much easier to evidence than *understand all the colours on a basic colour wheel.*

Before we move on to the next section, let's get something straight – we might not always agree with what the governmental agenda for education is. Shocking, I know – but that's the reality. However, this can, and often does, create a tension within your professional role that there is no easy solution to.

As a professional teacher employed, no matter how vicariously, by Central Government to deliver on their agenda, it falls to you to reconcile your personal and professional values and ethics with the demands of the industry.

Am I saying this is easy? No. But I am saying it is a consideration you must take seriously. Not all of those reading this will be in a publicly funded role, but if public money touches you at all, then you'll be in scope for an inspection and that will mean the scrutiny of the funding agencies.

It may help, albeit slightly, to adopt the stance that anything asked of you by an organisation is done so, not to complicate your life, but actually to ensure the overall impact on the teaching and learning is the best it can be, and these measures are in place to allow you to show off how well you do this.

Convinced? Well, I tried.

> ***REALITY CHECK:***
>
> ***Bear in mind that in most cases, the observer won't see the whole of your lesson.***
>
> ***Look at the observation report form used on your teacher-training course, and using a highlighter pick out all the criteria you can provide evidence for just through your session plan, scheme of work, and other standard teaching documentation (assessment records etc).***
>
> ***Consider how you might best present this to the observer then they arrive so they can find it easily, thus making their job – and yours – a little easier.***

Planning for Inclusive Teaching & Learning Approaches (including technology)

You may have noticed that this particular criterion as it actually appears is active in nature, considering that it requires the observer to confirm that you have *used* inclusive approaches. Well done if you thought that – it means you'll be great at writing your own criteria after all. And you're quite right; however, I'm taking the liberty of deploying artistic license for a moment, as before you use those approaches, you need to have planned for them.

It is so important when it comes to structuring your session plan, that you break it down; show the uninitiated reader each step to be taken, and make it clear when and how you are applying these inclusive approaches. It is also not a compromise of your professionalism to articulate within the session plan what makes them so inclusive. If you recall the range of key components one might expect to see when building a session plan, listed earlier in this chapter, there are aspects of equality to consider, as well as differentiation.

Often, trainee-teachers miss the opportunity to demonstrate how they have planned to ensure equality (either through adapted variations of activities, or resources, or the planned deployment of a Learning Support Assistant) thus making their teaching and learning approaches inclusive. Similarly, ensuring that individuals are catered for in terms of applying suitable stretch and challenge through the session is also often missed, with teachers opting instead to wing it, and throw in extra stuff if it's needed. Not the best way forward. Not remotely.

Because you know the different levels of ability within your group, given your initial assessment and your ongoing monitoring of their progress, it should be a standard part of your professional practice to ensure you are planning for individual needs and ability levels, even if you don't know the learners (e.g. one off workshops may cater to three ability levels).

This doesn't need to be excessively onerous, however. It may well be that you identify that you are setting specific groups within your session different tasks that are suited to their abilities, but ultimately all working towards the same objective, dovetailing together in the end. Alternatively, it could be that you have determined a set of differentiated questions that you intend to deploy through a nominated approach, thus ensuring control over who answers what, and utilizing your knowledge of their levels of appreciation and comprehension to effectively apply challenge on an individual level, with questions growing in complexity as you build on each answer and so target the more able.

The session plan can become the place you record this specific level of detail, thus demonstrating how you are inclusive by design, not by accident. Similarly, if you have had to adapt a resource to make it suitable for everyone to use, this should also be referenced. As a side note, do ensure that any visual resources are suitably representative of modern day culture – avoid stereotypical 'traditional' images that ignore changing demographics. Whatever your personal views, beliefs and politics, when you are a teacher, you need to embrace diversity in all of its forms, and actively celebrate it.

Your resources are an excellent place to start this, and something that will not only add enrichment to the learners' experience, but will support you in demonstrating more of your commitment to equality and diversity through your practice, which your observer will be delighted to witness.

Again, whilst this book is not intended to be a 'quick-fix' to passing your in-class observations, it is often useful to revisit some of these fundamental ways to ensure you are attending to inclusivity, equality and diversity. This is not a generalist educational textbook, the likes of which will include examples of generic approaches to these, and indeed, the kind you will probably use whilst working on your assignments, but in relation to supporting you in actively planning to acknowledge how you are taking these factors into account (to enhance both your ongoing professional delivery as well as helping you to be as prepared as possible for your observation) it is important that you look at examples.

The following case study is based on a real-life event. The setting is a community learning college, with several participants recently returning to education. Read through the event, and consider the questions posed below.

Case Study: Jamal's Cover Session

Jamal had been asked to cover a session for a colleague who was signed off as sick for the week. Rather than cancel the session, and disappoint the learners, the organisation approached Jamal to see if he would be happy to deliver the session, as it was a subject within his area of specialism (even though he was a relatively new teacher). Jamal agreed on the understanding he would have a copy of the regular teacher's session plan for class in advance, so he could be prepared. This was confirmed.

On the day of the session, Jamal arrived in good time and had prepared the hand-outs and presentation slides for the session. Once all of the learners had arrived, Jamal introduced himself and the observer, who was sitting unobtrusively to one side, and talked the learners through the objectives for the session, adhering to the session plan. He then picked up the pile of hand-outs he had prepared, and referring nervously to the session plan for clarification, asked the group "So which on of you has the dyslexia? I have the coloured hand-out for you here." After a couple of seconds, one of the learners, a middle-aged man, raised his hand, and Jamal asked one of the other learners to pass the coloured handout to the dyslexic learner.

Following the observation, Jamal explained to the observer that the session plan only alluded to the fact 'one learner had dyslexia so needed any printing on green paper' so – to be inclusive – he had prepared a specific set of the hand-outs on green, but the lesson plan failed to record to whom these needed to go, and consequently he felt a little embarrassed having to ask the class. The observer pointed out that he possibly wasn't as embarrassed as the learner who had been asked to raise his hand.

Points for consideration:

1. If you had been planning your session for someone to cover, how might you have recorded this particular situation more effectively in your plan to support the person covering your class?
2. If you were in Jamal's position, how might you have approached the situation more effectively, so that you didn't need to draw everyone's attention to his dyslexia (something he may not have wished to be shared widely)?
3. Reflect on your current courses; do you have any learners with specific support requirements? If so, how do you ensure that you are recording how you provide that support at a sessional level within your session plan? You may wish to discuss this with peers to gain a range of approaches.

Whilst planning to be inclusive in your teaching and learning approaches can, at times, be a little generic (as more often than not you'll already be ensuring your activities and methods never become exclusive), it is often in the deployment of resources and emergent technology that trainee teachers tend to fall down.

From a basic error such as Jamal's, whereby rather than simply give everyone the same colour handouts, thus ensuring inclusion, to something more complex, such as only using (for example) images of white middle class people within their presentations, trainees often miss opportunities to take proactive steps to incorporate examples that more accurately reflect modern society. Whilst the white middle classes have every right to be represented within your sessions, so too do other groups and individuals. Always consider alternative ways to embed diversity – once you start, you'll be surprised how many opportunities present themselves to you.

Resources in general need to be effectively planned for, whether this is the use of standard classroom equipment (such as an interactive white board, flip chart and so forth), or more specific technological equipment, such as tablets, or more creatively, the use of learners' own mobile devices, usually their smartphones.

Often teachers steer clear of incorporating the use of learners' phones in the session, and indeed some institutions object. However, centralising learners in the processes of learning and acquiring new knowledge can be so easily achieved by planning to let them use their phones in class. Within colleges, phone use is usually prohibited (as they can become a distraction in class), and some learners may challenge the no-use rule. This can be easily overcome by making the phones a resource in themselves. Setting in-class, individual or small group research tasks that require, for example, online research via their phones is a great, easy and inclusive method that places the onus of finding out and reporting back on the learners.

We will explore more approaches like this in the next chapter, but the key message here is to reference the use of the resources within your session plan; it is all too regularly a feature of incomplete session plans that the resources to be used in the session do not appear which, in turn, suggests to an observer that any associated issues have also not been taken into consideration.

Typical issues to take into account when planning to use inclusive resources are sufficiency (have you prepared enough for everyone who needs them?), accuracy (is the content up-to-date and/or grammatically correct?), suitability (do the resources extend the learning for everyone effectively?), representative (so where there are references to people, groups, events etc do they incorporate wider socio-cultural examples, and challenge racial and gender stereotypes). Don't fall into the lazy planner's trap of just using what you know about – investigate, and show off what you've found out! Remember, it is a clear part of the teacher's responsibility to reflect the wider world, and seamlessly build in these elements as a matter of course, into your course.

Top Tips & Bugbears – Advanced Planning

To conclude this chapter, let's pull together some of the frequently spotted errors, as well as tips provided directly from trainees who have gone through the observation process. Remember, the advance planning for your sessional observation isn't just recorded in your session plan; it's all the planning to ensure the visit runs smoothly, and that your observer has access to everything they need to know and see for them to have confidence in your meeting of the standards.

But let's start with the session plan, and those minor niggles that can be so easily avoided, but that sadly so frequently creep into otherwise perfectly sound sessions simply due to a lack of attention to detail, or thinking things through. These bugbears are drawn from both experienced observers as well as from feedback

Timings – they need to add up! It may sound oddly obvious, but one of the functions of the session plan is to support the teacher (you) in structuring the learning to fit in the time allowed. So whether this is a short micro-teach or a three-hour session, the timings need to demonstrate that you have planned to make the very best use of the time available. Not only this, however – accurate timings also reflects your ability to estimate and implement your conceptual awareness of how long tasks will last, which in turn provides evidence of your minimum core (time management is a numeracy skill, after all). How you represent timings can vary, and your organisation may have its own policy. Some teachers always prefer to use the actual times (so 09.30 Registration and H&S; 09.35 Warm-

Up Challenge Activity etc.), whereas some prefer to simply record the span of time (so in this case, 1-5mins Registration & H&S; 5-15mins Warm-Up Challenge Activity etc.). In some cases, just the duration is recorded (5mins Registration & H&S; 10mins Warm-Up Challenge Activity etc.), and in fairness there is no one true way. Speaking to observers who assess classroom teaching and learning, actual times tend to be preferred, as this allows the assessor to make clearer judgments about how well planned those timings are, and let's be pragmatic – if it makes your assessor's life easier, then it wouldn't hurt to find out their preferences (if they have one) and employ it.

Coming back to the original point – few things are as disappointing to find in a session plan than inaccurate timings; yes, sometimes activities can finish unexpectedly early, or may last longer if learners take more time than expected to engage with, or grasp, the demands of the task. Minor fluctuations can be allowed for, of course, but outright inaccuracies simply confound assessors. Another easy win when using the actual times in your session plan is that it is harder to make the error of miscalculating how much time is remaining. Believe me, there have been too many instances when teachers have used durations for activities that either mean the 'planned' lesson ends 15 minutes too early, or (in some ways worse) 35 minutes after the session should have finished. This screams hurried planning that has very little attention to detail, and attention to detail is important when teaching. You wouldn't accept such sloppiness from your learners, would you? Remember, this observation is an assessment of you!

Including meaningful learning objectives – the creation of learning objectives isn't easy, not least for less experienced teachers. We will look at phrasing learning objectives more in the next couple of chapters, as they can be used to set what learning will be taking place as well as giving you something tangible to assess against as well, but it would be remiss not to mention the all too frequent issue of insubstantial learning objectives here.

Framing learning objectives in such a way that they convey what you as the teacher are expecting your learners to achieve (and more so, *demonstrate* that they have achieved) is a key factor underpinning successful sessions. You need to be clear on what the session is setting out to provide in terms of new learning and ensure that the content relates to this. Often, assessors see very vague learning objectives (*'This session will explore Newton's three laws of motion'*) that mean very little in terms of actual learning outcomes – remember, the objective(s) of the session will almost always have a direct correlation to the planned outcomes, by which I mean that new learning that your learners will have acquired by the end of the class. Remember, also, that you need to stretch you learners by challenging them throughout the session so let your objectives support you in that. Be specific – let the objectives support you in recognising in your planning that different learners will achieve different levels of engagement and acquisition. This also allows you to plan for in-class assessment activities that are directly linked to your expectations. Again, more on this is to follow shortly, but when composing learning objectives, just re-read them and ask yourself if they are sufficiently specific to be measurably achieved within the class.

Covering all bases – This might sound a bit vague in itself, but actually it is ensuring you take full advantage of knowing what the criteria are for these observation, and making sure you use it. There is no excuse, knowing that assessors are looking at how you plan for specific things, for not planning for it! These assessments are not surprise visits – they are negotiated, so you know we are coming.

One of my recent trainees told me that *'I make sure to write out in full all the Equality & Diversity, English & maths, and how I am differentiating between learners – this was very time consuming to start with and involved a lot of lateral thinking in order to be creative with different ways to meet the criteria, but I got into the habit of writing better sessions plans!'*

This is pleasing to hear, as the practices learned during the course should manifest in your day-to-day teaching life forever, ideally. Yes, we agreed earlier it can take time, especially at the beginning of this journey, but it gets easier as you become accustomed to working like this. Being observed will continue beyond the completion of your teacher training, as it is a core quality assurance and improvement tool, so learn good habits now. Make direct reference to learners' needs (and what you're doing to meet them), make clear how you intend to assess aspects of the new learning.

A side question to this that I get asked is – when referring to learners with specific circumstances or additional needs – whether or not their names can (or indeed should) appear in the lesson plan. Firstly, there may be a local policy about this, so that is the first port of call for you. If one is not present, then my advice is to use initials. The session plan isn't a public document, so learners should never really see it (so anonymity is secure), and you'll know to whom you are referring. From an assessor's perspective, this shows you planning to be inclusive, but also they can cross-reference the initials with your assessment records (which will include some reference to that which lies beneath your planning for differentiation) thus ensuring your planning reflects assessment information, and take it into account.

Identifying the teacher's role – don't forget 'you'! Too often, what the teacher is doing at any given point can be neglected; include what you have planned for yourself, whether it is leading a demonstration of how to create a wedding bouquet, or that you are hovering around the room to monitor individual progress and provide guidance and feedback. Don't lose sight of yourself (similarly, but less frequent, don't forget to be clear on what you're expecting the learners to be doing at any given point either!).

Don't bunch, chunk – consider the level of detail you provide. It is not great to bunch several things together into a single 25 minute block, especially if a lot if planned to go on. Instead, chuck the learning more leanly – can those 25 minutes be broken into a 5 minute introduction, 10 minute learner activity, 10 minute plenary on the task and then 5 minutes to reflect on the new learning? If so, do it! It's better to follow and much clearer for your observer to see your thinking.

Finally, and perhaps one of the most irksome errors about planning and session plans – actually have one! As mentioned, these observations are arranged in conjunction with you, so you know we are coming. You know a large part of your assessment being successful depends upon you having planned an inclusive session, and you know we have to see it. Not having one for your assessor is self-sabotaging, so please don't do it. It is in your power to make this work for you, to show off so much of your planning and you delivery skill – don't throw that opportunity away.

In the next chapter, we will consider the essential criteria linked to learning, and how you can best demonstrate this to your assessors whilst providing your learners with the very best learning experience possible.

4 LEARNING, LEARNING, LEARNING!

This Chapter will focus on how the teacher ensures new learning is taking place, and the key aspects of delivery that will ensure the learners are making progress; it will consider the role of resources in the overall delivery of learning, and how exactly teachers can present their flexibility during class.

This Chapter relates to the following Professional Standards:

Professional values and attributes – *(1) Evaluate what works best in your teaching and learning to meet the diverse needs of your learners; (2) Evaluate and challenge your practice, values and beliefs; (3) Inspire, motivate and raise expectations for learners through your enthusiasm and knowledge; (4) Be creative and innovative in selecting and adapting strategies to help learners to learn; (5) Value and promote social and cultural diversity, equality of opportunity and inclusion; (6) Build positive and collaborative relationships with colleagues and learners*

Professional knowledge and understanding – *(7) Maintain and update knowledge of your subject and/or vocational area; (9) Apply theoretical understanding of effective practice in teaching, learning and assessment drawing on research and other evidence; (10) Evaluate your practice with others to assess its impact on* *learning; (11); Manage and promote positive learner behaviour; (12) Understand the teaching and professional role and your responsibilities*

Professional skills – *(13) Motivate and inspire learners to promote achievement and develop their skills to enable progression; (14) Plan and deliver effective learning programmes for diverse groups; (15) Promote the benefits of technology and support learners in its use; (16) Address the mathematics and English needs of learners, and work creatively to overcome individual barriers to learning; (17) Enable learners to share responsibility for their own learning and assessment, setting goals that stretch and challenge*

Learning is the name of our game. As such, it is no surprise that so much of the observation focuses upon the business of learning. These next two chapters look at both aspects of this – Chapter 5 will explore the role of assessment in the teaching and learning cycle of your delivery, and this chapter will cover how you ensure new learning is taking place and meeting all those individual needs you've identified previously.

It is very easy, especially in the early stages of a teaching career, to fall into the trap that what you want to teach is what your students want to learn – this isn't always the case, and often teachers have to make some adaptations to their own expectations and perceptions; meeting learners needs is one thing, but actually meeting the needs of awarding bodies or indeed your employer(s) can unexpectedly be at odds with what you may have initially thought you'd be teaching, and indeed how you'd be teaching it. Constraints on time, the pressures of awarding body criteria (if applicable to you and your courses) can weigh heavily on what you can or cannot include in your course. This should be something that your employer can support you with, but the key word in this is 'expectation.'

Your expectations for your learners need to be consistently high; of course learners will all have varying ability levels – that's a given, but it doesn't stop you having only the highest expectations for each and every one of them – and yes, that may vary from learner to learner, and so it should. Remember – we are talking about meeting individual needs, and the very ethos of education and training is that each learner, no matter their existing level of skill, knowledge and ability, deserves their teacher to challenge them to the limits of their potential, and maybe beyond.

This should permeate through all of your planning, but also in your delivery; indeed it is in the execution of your teaching and learning sessions that the sense of your expectation can be truly communicated – your demeanour, your attitude, every aspect of your delivery should exude that high expectation. This sets up, very quickly, an atmosphere conducive to truly outstanding teaching and learning. Is this explicit in any teacher training criteria? Nope. But as an important attitudinal approach, if it isn't burning within you, then it is very hard to elevate your performance in the following criteria from the mechanistic to the artistic. Do think about the expectations you have for your learners – and never lose sight of that throughout your career. We'll touch on this a little more shortly, but given how significant our learners are, it was worth introducing this idea here.

In the meantime, let's take a look at the learning-focused criteria you need to evidence during your observations:

- *Confirm how the candidate has established and sustained a safe inclusive learning environment*
- *Confirm how the candidate has used inclusive teaching and learning approaches and resources to meet the individual needs of learners*
- *Confirm how the candidate has communicated with learners to meet individual learning needs*
- *Confirm how the candidate has demonstrated ways to*

promote equality and value diversity in own teaching
- *Confirm how the candidate has designed resources that actively promote (a) equality and value diversity and (b) meet the needs of specific learners*
- *Confirm how the candidate has demonstrated flexibility and adaptability in the use of inclusive teaching and learning approaches and resources*

Over the next few pages, we will examine each of these criteria. Some, like jigsaw pieces, fit together effortlessly and can evidenced in conjunction with each other. Some are a little more complex, so we will look at those in isolation.

REALITY CHECK:

Reflect on your last session, and look at your session plan too if that helps.

(i) **What 'new' learning took place in that session? What took place that extended the reach of your learners' skills, knowledge and/or abilities to beyond where they were at the start of the lesson? Did the learners recognise this fresh acquisition of new learning?**

(ii) **How much 'new' learning are you intending to generate in your next session? Will your learners be able to articulate what they can do at the end of the session they couldn't at the start?**

Setting the Scene: Your Learning Environment

The hub of your teaching and learning activity, the learning environment can take on many forms. Traditionally, it can be a classroom but in reality it can be a multitude of spaces – a workshop, a garage, a beauty salon, a library, a florists, a hospital, a computer suite; arguably, the list is practically endless. Indeed, with so many 'home-study' options available, such as online courses, or CDs that potential students can listen to and learn from the comfort of their own home or car, the fact learners elect to join a programme where attendance is required needs to be acknowledged.

Indeed, for many learners returning to education after a break, that decision can be momentous. They may be feeling vulnerable, exposed, and may have very mixed historical feelings about their prior learning experiences; not everyone can say that school was the best days of their lives, after all. Whilst you might not have access to all of that information prior to the first time you meet them, you can take it as read that anyone joining a new course for the first time will have some degree of apprehension, and some more than others.

With this in mind, what can you do to make them feel safe in their class? The learning environment, after all, is your domain, and it is your responsibility to make sure that your learners feel at ease within it. Why? Because you're naturally considerate and benevolent? Possibly that's part of it, but from a teaching and learning perspective, a welcoming and nurturing environment is essential to ensure that your learners feel suitably comfortable so that they might engage to their fullest potential.

To support this, we do need to look briefly at a little bit of theory and, in all honesty, it is probably theory you have already heard mentioned within your own teacher training courses. This particular element of theory is one that is often introduced in pretty loose terms to trainees without them having to really engage too much in what it 'looks like' in real life.

I'm referring to Maslow's famed *hierarchy of needs* (1970), which is often depicted as a pyramid or a triangle. Feel free to explore this further using any online search engine you fancy. We're not bothered about the aesthetics here, rather we want to consider what each progressive layer of the hierarchy looks like in action.

As a quick recap, Abraham Maslow was an American psychologist and whilst exploring the nature of human motivation, conceptualised the series of physiological requirements – or needs – that people to feel able to work effectively to their optimum potential. This has transferred into the received wisdom of educational professionals as being a template for consideration when developing the learning environment in such as way as to make it as conducive to learning as possible.

Let's reflect on the progressive elements Maslow constructed, and think about what this looks like for us as teachers:

Physiological needs – the foundation layer of the hierarchy, these relate to very basic human needs such as warmth, comfort, food/drink. Arguably, learners are unlikely to be eating or drinking in our lessons, but the place needs to be at least comfortable. This is often associated with temperature and the furniture, but think also about the placement of the furniture. Can everyone see where and what they need to without straining? Is there a clear line of sight to you from where you are seating them? This really is a key foundation layer to be aware of when establishing a safe learning environment – the learners have to feel comfortable in the most basic of ways. Access to toilet facilities is another consideration, as is physical access (consider if any of your learners have restricted mobility, for example – is the room accessible in every way for them?).

Safety needs – for this, are the learners clear on evacuation procedures, and associated muster points? Have they had a fire drill? Are they confident you know what to do in the event of an emergency? In more generic teaching terms, have you ensured that any health and safety information has been effectively communicated (and reiterated) to the learners? Many lessons have no subject specific health and safety information, but anything using IT equipment, for example, may require reminders on correct posture and placement of the screen, as well as placing drinks near the wires etc. Similarly craft courses can often use sharp edges or require protective clothing – yes, some of this may well be common sense, but it is still the responsibility of the teacher to ensure that learners are educated in what is required and reminded to follow expected safety processes. Is the room itself safe, with no trailing wires or exposed fuses, or broken windows? Similarly, are the learners aware of the local safeguarding and Prevent Duty procedures? We'll look at this in more detail momentarily.

Acceptance & Belonging – these make reference to the learners' place in the group. There is a lot of theory out there around supporting group development and cohesion, and some of it is well worth a look. As the leader of the class, the teacher should be considering how best to ensure their cohort blend as well as they could so that individuals feel able to contribute without fear of (needless) criticism, and participate openly in activities. Learners need to feel part of the whole, and this can be achieved through the use of many strategies. Getting learners to use each other's names as early as possible is a good technique for this (and requires that you as the teacher do it, too). Setting up activities that allows learners to nominate the next one to answer, for example, builds this, and also supports the group bonding in situations of low-level stress that requires them to work together. Only very low levels are advised, as you don't want them stressed to the point that the earlier aspects of the hierarchy are compromised!

Self-esteem – this is the tier where the learners begin to recognise that you, and their peers, see value in their contributions and that – as a result of the previous layer being achieved – confidence begins to develop that lends its own support to the learners' ongoing development and expansion in terms of their learning, and feeling about to take an active role in it. It is easy to observe in classes where learners do not feel able to participate in a session, either because other learners routinely dominate discussions, or even worse, the teacher frequently closes them down and fails to use any effective praising techniques to build them up. This all contributes to the safety of the learning environment, and ultimately leads to...

Self-actualisation – the pinnacle of the hierarchy, the achievement of 'self-actualisation' can manifest in many ways, but for the here and now let's classify it as the learner developing autonomy. This may be only around an aspect of the work, or it may be complete. This is nothing for teachers to fret about; quite the reverse – after all, everything you've been doing is really, if you think about it, to enable the learners to do what you have taught them without you there! That is, after all, probably why they are attending in the first place.

This may sound somewhat overly complex, but it really isn't – a lot of it is common sense, and as an empathetic teacher you'll no doubt be ensuring much if not all of this is in place as a matter of course. But don't hide your light under a bushel; remember your assessor needs to observe that you make the classroom a safe place, so show it off.

> **REALITY CHECK:**
>
> **Consider the various stages of Maslow's Hierarchy of Needs.**
>
> **(i) Reflect on your last lesson, and consider how safe the environment was, but using those headings as a lens**
>
> **(ii) Taking it a stage further, turn those headings into a checklist, and under each write out exactly what you have put in place – or maybe could put in place – to ensure you are pro-actively taking planned steps to make the environment a safe place for all**

In addition to applying the above, you will also have local policies to adhere to, and as such will definitely have to make your learners aware of the Safeguarding & Prevent Duty protocols for your organisation.

Safeguarding legislation was introduced to encourage mutli-agency working to support the protection of all learners (and staff) irrespective of age or vulnerable status. This is a vast subject, and one you will cover on your teacher training programme, but reminding your learners of the local policy, and the lines of contact for the designated Safeguarding Officer, is not only useful for creating that safe environment, but also for ensuring your learners have every opportunity to disclose any issues they may have.

Similarly, the introduction of the Prevent Duty as part of the Counter-Terrorism and Security Act (2015) sees all in public roles tasked with the need for vigilance around those at risk (or potential risk) of marginalisation, possibly making them vulnerable to radicalisation and susceptible to extremist narratives. Often aligned with safeguarding in many institutions, the Prevent Duty agenda is something that cannot be overlooked, and teachers are encouraged to tackle any in-class topics professionally but whilst challenging perceptions and views. Your own institution will have guidance on this, and probably professional development training available. If you are unsure about it, your first port of call needs to be the designated safeguarding officer at your organisation.

The last point I'll make under the safe and inclusive learning environment is one of introductions. Whilst it may seem trite, observers are very keen that teachers introduce them to the class. This is not an ego-related thing (at least, it shouldn't be...) but rather one of putting the learners at ease. Remember, they may only just be getting comfortable with you and their peers; having a stranger in the room typing or scribbling away can be very disconcerting, so put them out of their misery, and de-mystify the stranger in the corner.

The absence of this may make learners reluctant to participate freely, and does nothing for the development of that safe environment. You don't have to tell them they are observing your lesson as part of your teaching qualification if you feel that undermines you, but tell them something. After all, chances are there will be a few observations coming along, so it's much better to get them on side, and don't have them worrying. Plus, it can be a good rehearsal just in case Ofsted comes to call!

Using Inclusive Teaching & Learning Approaches

Having ensured you have a safe learning environment, both on an emotional and physical level, there comes the business of teaching and learning. This is what you have planned for, the use of a range of activities that will allow you to successfully transmit new learning (be it knowledge or skills based) to your group. The volume and range of delivery methods are many and varied, and no doubt something that you will have explored in class on your teacher training programme.

The scope of the delivery methods available, and their effectiveness, are all factors that you'll need to consider when it comes to structuring the planned learning for any given session. After all, not every delivery approach is likely to be most appropriate. You may also want to consider some of the key theories behind learning, and learning styles, by way of justifying your choices. Remember – your approaches need to be inclusive, but in fairness, this should not really be something you struggle with, especially if you ask yourself a few key questions when determining your methods/approaches of choice:

1. *Does this delivery method make best use of all of the learners and extend their knowledge/skills on the topic being covered?*
2. *Can all learners actively participate in the planned activity without any potential difficulties arising as a result of support requirements? If not, can the whole activity be adjusted reasonably to ensure this is resolved, or can the activity be structured so that different learners engage in a range of different ways?*
3. *Whilst all activities should stretch and challenge everyone as is appropriate to their own needs and level of ability, is it clear how the activity is differentiated to allow this to happen meaningfully?*
4. *Does this approach/activity make engaging with the*

> *learning memorable and interesting? These two features are essential in maintaining learner motivation, not to mention your own!*

I mentioned earlier about taking learning styles into consideration, as well as other theories surrounding how people learn. There are many schools of thought surrounding learning styles, and this is an area of study you'll cover during your training. Whilst we won't delve too deeply here, we will take a moment to recognise the most vital aspect – people all learn differently.

Or do they? Perhaps it would be more correct to state that people have a preference to how they like to learn. Some prefer to watch, others prefer to get their hands dirty and learn by doing. Building on the established work of Kolb (1984) and his learning styles model, Honey and Mumford (1986) identified four 'learner types' and classified these as *Activists, Pragmatists, Reflectors*, and *Theorists*. These were derived from the dominant characteristic of the learner type, and are admittedly quite colourfully drawn, however – their dominant characteristic is still just that, dominant amongst others.

It is a recurring trainee-teacher's pitfall to accept that learning styles should overtly dictate the way one plans one's learning sessions – if you have identified, for sake of argument, that you have a mix of Activist learners in with Theorists (please note, other schools of thought are available), then do you only select teaching and learning approaches that cater to these two learner-types? I sincerely hope not.

Part of the remit of a good teacher is to broaden the horizons of any learner, not necessarily just educationally, but also as an individual. As such, to limit one's learners to their own preferences is to limit the creative palette that is learning overall. No, the fact that individuals may have a preferred way of learning merely tells us that they may be under-exposed to other approaches, or that they had poor prior learning experiences. We have the skills and artistry to introduce them to a range of learning approaches that will not only extend their learning but also their ability to learn. The possibilities for them to make significant gains in their own learning through engagement with a lot of previously untried (by them) methods may be a little unsettling at first, but due to the safe and nurturing environment you have created, they will feel secure enough to rise to such challenges, and your lessons will be the more interesting and exciting for it.

The nature of teaching and learning approaches should also be considered for a moment. As ever, education-speak can leave us a little unclear when it comes to what we're actually talking about. Approaches could be understood in many ways, but what do we really mean? Well, for us the approach we adopt is usually the method we select to use, either in isolation or in conjunction with other methods and resources, to communicate the new learning. Whether we call them methods, or activities, or approaches, we are essentially discussing the practical media through which you deliver learning.

Are some methods better than others? Arguably yes; few people put much stock by pure lecturing these days. Stereotypically dull and disconnected, lecturing is a very 'old-school' approach to delivery but, that said, there may be some aspects of your content that – in closely managed moderation – a lecture approach may best serve. And that's the rub; how are your topics, and indeed the learners, best served? This is where your professional judgment and choice come into play as on this score it is hard to provide a formulaic answer. What works for one won't always work for another, but never shy away from experimentation as a teacher – you'll surprise yourself by what you can come up with.

That said, of course, there already exists quite the compendium of learning methods that we can consider when looking at how best to ensure our teaching and learning is as inclusive, and indeed as meaningful, as possible. Below, we can consider some of the more frequently used, and in doing so think about how effectively different approaches place the learners at the centre of the learning process:

Presentation – not to be confused with an overly animated lecture, the use of presentation has a couple of applications. Firstly, it is an interactive means of transmitting new learning concepts to your audience, usually involving visual media (often, but not exclusively, presentation software such as PowerPoint or Keynote). Presentations are arguably the evolution of the dry approach historically associated with dusty old lecture halls that were far too insular and teacher-centred. Educational thinking has moved on considerably, the disengaging pure lecture is hopefully a thing of the past. In terms of learner-centrality, presentations undertaken by the teacher still err towards being teacher-centric, but if we consider the second use, we can flip that around. Presentations can be an approach that places learners directly at the centre of them, by getting them to do the presenting. Indeed, presentations can be useful mechanisms to allow learners the chance to feed back (individually or collaboratively) on their views, understanding or findings, depending on what you have set them to complete. This also allows the teacher the opportunity to factor in some assessment, and possibly even peer assessment.

Demonstration – always very valuable in practical sessions, the demonstration is useful in showing learners how best to complete specific tasks, skills, actions etc. There are numerous applications for the demonstration, but key is the skill of the teacher in making the demonstration clear, with well-defined instructions for following the required sequence of actions to complete the aim of the activity. Once again, the centralising of the learners in a demonstration can vary depending on how the activity is conducted. For example, if the demonstration is purely 'teacher shows, learners watch,' then it remains very teacher-centric. However, this may well be the best approach to adopt, especially if there are safety considerations, perhaps. On the other hand, it may be appropriate to structure the demonstration so that either (i) the various elements are broken into segments, thus allowing the learners to duplicate the required aspects bit by bit, in turn reducing the amount of time they are inactive and just watching, or indeed (ii) the demonstration allows for simultaneous participation of the learners, so making it much more 'teacher shows, learners duplicate' – but, as a cautionary note, do ensure when following this method that all learners can see what you are doing clearly, and that you can see them to provide corrective feedback as required. Having high expectations is very important, but learners cannot reasonably undertake complex tasks without first having the opportunity to learn the component parts.

Discussion – A good discussion is always a worthwhile aspect of a learning session, but how are we defining 'good' here? Firstly, a good discussion is well managed, and allows for all learners to participate appropriately. It should be contained to the topic or topics that are in focus, and any tangents emerging should only be explored if you as the teacher deem them an appropriate extension of the core topic. It is perfectly acceptable for you to re-focus a discussion, by telling the learners you'll pick on these emerging thoughts at a later point (assuming that you will!). Discussions are excellent approaches for exploring important themes and topics, and can be used skillfully by teachers to elicit levels of prior attainment as well as extending current levels of knowledge by getting them to thrash ideas and concepts out as a whole class. This is a very learner-centric activity, but heavily dependent on effective classroom management.

Debate – Not used as often as it could be, debates are frequently incorrectly believed to be the same as discussions. This is not the case, and sadly results in opportunities to really challenge learners being missed. Very learner-centric when executed correctly, debates allow learners the scope to flex their intellectual muscles as well as develop quick thinking skills and forcing them to engage under acceptable levels of pressure with the core learning topics. When set up correctly, the teacher acts as the Chair of the debate setting the motion (by which we mean the contentious point that the two groups will debate), but otherwise the learners should feel in the driving seat. The class would be divided into two, and would be issued opposing views – one arguing for the motion, the other arguing against. This also allows learners to consider wider perspectives than the view they would necessarily automatically adopt. In preparation, once the motion is shared, each group has around 10-15 minutes to prepare their argument, with their speaking order determined by them, or by the teacher – the opening speaker sets the nature of their perspective (so why they do or do not agree with the motion), with the view that the last speaker recaps all the salient points emerging, as well as summing up the their team's argument. Each person has 2 minutes to speak, alternating one at a time between the teams, and the challenge is to (i) advance the team's argument whilst (ii) rebuffing their opposite number's argument as best they can. Of course, part of the trick is to anticipate the opposing arguments and be ready for them but, as it isn't completely predictable, they must be responsive to what they hear. This may sound challenging to manage and implement, but it really isn't. Teachers do shy away from applying debate activities, and this is such a shame. The benefits for the learners can be significant.

In-class research – Slightly smaller scale than managing a debate, but still very learner-centred, setting up in-class research puts the onus of the learning squarely with the class. Whether they are using computers, or you make effective use of their own internet enabled devices, setting learners some in-class research means they are taking responsibility for aspects of their own learning, and also affords them the opportunity of sharing their findings; this can require effective time management skills, as well as note taking and skim reading; all in all, a handy task for also developing some of their English and maths skills as well as placing them at the very centre of their own learning through investigation. This also allows you the additional option of differentiating the nature and complexity of the research topic to suit those to whom you give it, ensuring all are challenged appropriately throughout.

Composite tasks – this can take many forms, and in some ways is an extension of a few different approaches, but one that specifically capitalises upon your learners' mixed and varied abilities. Composite tasking requires the teacher to plan a range of tasks, varying in the level of technical demand and/or complexity required to complete them, that either interlink, or build upon one another, thus allowing for whole class practical activity which is working towards the same goal or topic, but with differentiated component parts. Through this approach, all learners are challenged appropriately to their level of ability, whilst never singling anyone out or demotivating them through poorly presented activities that highlight skills and knowledge deficiencies rather than promotes the extension of their learning. This kind of activity does require significant forethought by the teacher, but pays off with an array of interconnected and learner-driven outcomes.

Pair & Small Group Work – something of a sweeping, umbrella term, but the value of exploiting the group work of 3s/4s, or even pairs, shouldn't be underestimated. Learners tasked with exploring, defining, sharing understanding, considering impact, prompting prior learning, developing ideas/solutions and so forth in small groups is very effective. Subliminal competition kicks in, and learners want (in most cases) to both do well, and impress; impress you, and also their peers. Remember – this is part of establishing that safe learning environment, so you can combine the work you're doing with them to build this environment. Plus, the creativity and inventiveness of learners can often be surprising, not least to them!

> **REALITY CHECK:**
>
> **Reflect on your last session, looking at your choice and range of learning activities**
>
> (i) *How much of the time was spent with you overtly 'leading' the proceedings? 70%? 80%? Could you revise the activities used to put more emphasis on the learners' centrality?*
>
> (ii) *Consider your next session – look at the activities you're electing to use and consider how much of the time the learners are actually at the heart of it. If it is less than 50%, could you adapt your approaches to give them more of a lead?*

Your session is more than just the range of activities you are deploying, of course – never forget that you need to maintain the overarching attention to inclusivity in your approaches, and how you are using them to meet individual need.

Have you considered the layout of the room? Not just the arrangement of the tables/desks and equipment, but also the dispersal of learners? Remember – this is your classroom, and you can direct the activity that goes on, and this includes the seating arrangement. Many teachers don't consider the seating arrangement has much of an impact on the quality of the teaching and learning experience, but I would beg to differ. Learners will slip into a pattern of sitting in their self-determined comfort zones, and, consequently, will forever be with their emerging friendship groups, for example.

This may not automatically present to you as an issue of inclusion, but what if you had a learner with a visual, or a hearing, impairment? What if they needed to have a specific seating location in the room – what do you do? If someone with a visual impairment had to sit facing you and the projection screen in order to engage, what do you do to ensure they sit where they need? Tell others they can't sit there because X needs it to see? Or perhaps a hearing impaired student needs to sit at the end of a horseshoe arrangement so they can effectively lip read both you and all the others; again, do you block off the seat to ensure they are able to be placed where they need so they can participate?

Seating arrangements are such a wonderfully simple approach to manage classroom behaviour, support group cohesion, ensure inclusivity through placements and set up specific differentiated groups to allow for stretch and challenge without lots of additional chaotic moving around. With name tag place-holders you, as the teacher, can situate learners exactly where you want them – or need them – to be without question. You can ensure peer support is set up in advance, or you can manage the placement of those who need to sit in specific locations in order to access the proceedings. Remember, if you routinely move everyone else, they are less likely to notice that one or two people are frequently in the exact same place, thus not drawing unwarranted attention to individuals. You can instigate pre-planned small group composition, and ensure that ability levels are mixed up, or brought together, depending on the focus of the tasks and the topic.

Read through the following case study regarding Andi's session, and then consider the questions arising from it. It may be worth reflecting on some of the points discussed earlier, too.

Case Study: Andi's ESOL Class

Andi spent a long time planning to be inclusive for her English for Speakers of Other Languages (ESOL) class, as she had been finding the cohort quite challenging. The group had first met five weeks ago, and already were forming small cliques within the wider class. This was leading to some repeated in-class chatter as well as Andi having to repeatedly request that her learners moved seats for the essential role plays that she has been using.

For this session, Andi is introducing the concept of formal and informal registers when communicating and wants to make sure that some of those learners less able to grasp concepts swiftly are supported by their peers, but she is aware that typically the friendship groups that have formed tend to reflect similar ability levels. Additionally, Andi has prepared a detailed presentation on the nuances of formal and informal speech. She had wanted to include a video to demonstrate these but couldn't find one to use that was suited to the mixed level of ability in the class. Instead, Andi is going to provide some explanations with a few readings interspersed in the presentation to demonstrate the differences.

Initially, this goes well but it becomes apparent that the two more capable huddles of learners are clearly following the topic clearly, and openly undertake their own comedic demonstrations of formal and informal, which entertains the whole class. This raises an unexpected point about emphasis and inference, which particularly confuses a few of those present. It arises when one learner picks up on the comedic demonstration using the same sentence twice, but the way it was said not only changed the level of formality, but also the meaning. One of the more advanced learners pointed out that several of Andi's examples on the interactive white board also could have other interpretations. Andi began to feel like the lesson was slipping away from her, and could see the body language of the less confident learners conveying significant confusion.

Poor Andi! Of course, unexpected topics can arise at any time and can generate curiosity in our learners (which isn't necessarily any bad thing), however in this case it seems to be a little unwelcome. Consider the following points:

1. Andi intended to use presentation and demonstration to explore the topic of formal and informal registers with her ESOL learners. Was this the best choice, or could this have been augmented/improved by considering other methods? If so, what and why?
2. The use of video to support delivery can be useful, as we'll explore shortly, so it was a shame Andi couldn't find anything suitable. Can you find any videos online that might have helped her?
3. Do you believe that the management of the classroom is as effective as it could be? What might you recommend to Andi that she could do moving forwards to support her in this?
4. The associated topic of inference and emphasis is an important one, but it seemed to be confusing some of the less confident learners. How could this have been tackled to both manage the situation and maximise the learning opportunity provided? What would you have done if a similar tangent had developed in your own session?

It isn't always possible to predict what will happen in a teaching session, no matter how much planning one undertakes. That said, a good teacher would be mindful of some potential outcomes that could arise, especially if choosing to present specific information. The teacher in the above example has made a few strategic faux pas, sadly, starting with not making effective use of a planned seating arrangement to manage the emerging cliques to start with.

Similarly, if the learners could recognise that the examples being used could have multiple connotations depending on emphasis, then so too should the teacher when planning. Attention to detail is so important when constructing a lesson, and as such you must take some time to reflect back on what you have planned to ensure you look at it with dispassionate eyes – the secret to doing this well is allowing yourself time; don't simply plan tomorrow's lesson tonight, get ahead of the tide and put a little distance between the point of delivery and when you are planning that session. Then you have time to park it, and go back to it prior to delivery for a once over.

With fresh eyes, you may be surprised at the things you spot that can either be used deliberately to start new conversations, or can be removed to ensure those conversations only start when you want them to. It's a professional choice, and it's *your* professional choice.

This ESOL class may also have benefitted from some clearly defined learning objectives/outcomes, as this would allow the teacher the opportunity to pull the class back to the intention of this session, and leave the door open to return to those other, very valid, discussions at a later point.

Learning outcomes are very important in demonstrating what learners should be gaining within a lesson; more than the aims (or pious hopes) of the teacher's delivery, the outcomes, or objectives, of the session should outline key milestones of the learning journey, but also allow for the learners to demonstrably achieve them.

In Chapter 5 we'll look in much more detail at the value and importance of well-defined learning objectives, and how they not only help shape the session, but also support effective assessment of learning.

Resourcing your learning: the tangible touch of equality & diversity

The advancement of learning can usually be successfully achieved by the use of resources to help stimulate interest in the topic, or lend additional support to the activities underway. It may be useful to make a few minor distinctions when it comes to talking about resources that may also help you when constructing your sessions.

Resources are not methods – this is a key point that inexperienced teachers often get muddled over. Methods (or learning strategies or teaching approaches, call them what you will) are the well-designed activities and channels through which you impart the new learning to your eager students. Resources are tangible artefacts that are deployed wisely by the teacher to enhance the learning approaches used, and contribute to making the activities work, the learning itself more memorable or, ideally, both.

Equipment is not quite the same as a resource – a little nit-picky, admittedly, but classroom equipment tends not to be the same as a learning resource. By classroom equipment I'm talking here about the likes of an interactive whiteboard, or a flipchart, or marker pens and such like. Basically, the general equipment one would realistically be able to anticipate most modern learning environments would naturally provide.

Resources can take many forms – and this is the important bit; some of the most outstanding sessions I have observed have made excellent use of the unexpected, the every-day, the 'normal' to enhance and re-enforce the new learning that is taking place. Yes, some classes may need to use online resources that are linked directly to the topic, but the artful teacher considers how to bring the outside world and the learning together. I have seen teachers use a range of non-traditional physical items to help illustrate the learning, whether they have taken the shape of items from a weekly domestic shopping trip, or homemade playing cards that reflect the topic, or indeed they are used to represent specific elements within a topic, to demonstrate how the aspects inter-relate. The application of creative thinking when it comes to creating new resources is boundless.

In all seriousness, many trainees feel that 'resources' simply applies to a set of presentation slides, some handouts and maybe a set of homemade flash cards (more on these in a moment). Actually, the sky is the limit when it comes to creating new resources to advance the learning in your sessions, and no, contrary to popular belief, you don't need a massive budget to achieve them.

Many successful resources produced by teachers capitalise on their simplicity (of the resources, that is, not the teachers). In a lot of ways, the tighter the budget, the more creative the teacher can get. Often it is sadly the case that organisations cannot purchase or overly support the creation of specific resources, and it falls to the teacher to generate these. Necessity is, as they say, the mother of invention, and teaching (as fewer say) is the midwife. The drive of a teacher to look for innovative ways to convey aspects of their subject through activities that revolve around the use of learning resources gives birth to many and varied items that can support the classroom delivery.

Let's take a quick moment to look at just a few possible homemade resources that can really help stimulate, advance and consolidate learning:

Flash Cards – mentioned earlier, and often associated with language learning, they usually take the form of a set of cards with either pictures or words (or both) that are shown to learners to check their attainment. However, this concept has been widely adapted into many subjects to act as a way of simulating conversations, and peer discussions. Easy to create, all you need is access to a computer and a printer, and some card. Ideally, these benefit from being laminated, which your organisation should be able to help you with, to ensure they remain durable.

Randomiser – similar to a 'spin-the-arrow' type creation, a rotating pointer fixed to a piece of card with a paper fastener to allow it to spin can be used for several purposes. It could be used by learners to assign tasks to themselves as part of a larger activity, or it could be used to assign questions, or the order of participating in a larger task. Some teachers have opted to create a digital randomiser, using easy to find online applications, but sometimes the use of something more 'hands-on' adds to the dynamic in the class.

Prompts & Clues – another laminated affair, but the use of cards with prompts for action to be taken, or specific in-class research, or even a series of clues that you may have located, much like a treasure hunt, around your learning space to encourage active movement and interaction away from simply setting instructions – getting learners up, and involving them in locating a series of tasks to be completed may seem a little silly, but the impact on an otherwise dry and immobile subject and group can be notable. Indeed, when often asked how to make a very dry subject more interesting and engaging, my response would almost always be to find another way for the learners to gather the information they need. Nothing screams 'this is a dry topic' louder than the dry delivery of a teacher! Pinning the onus onto the learners to investigate aspects of the topic independently completely changes that dynamic.

Common to the design and use of all resources is the need for them to be inclusive. At the very least, they need to not be 'exclusive' to anyone. The introduction of physical elements to the learning process can offer a range of terrific opportunities but as teachers we mustn't ever lose sight of the potential for these to actually add a barrier to participation. As such, we need to ask ourselves some questions about the resources we are electing to use:

1. Can all my learners engage with the resource? *By this, consider if the learners have any physical, cognitive or sensory conditions that might impact on their ability to engage effectively. If there is a potential barrier arising here, consider how you could circumvent it.*
2. Is the resource adaptable to ensure fair access for all? *Perhaps the resource itself can be adapted, either physically, or indeed in the way in which it can be used to support the learning. It may be that you can have the same resource but used in different ways by different in-class groups to ensure everyone can participate.*
3. Does the resource reflect the current world view? *This may seem like an odd one, but if you are creating resources (or choosing to use pre-existing ones) then are they representative of 21st century life – or do they instead promote a range of what once may have been considered 'traditional' images? Do the resources challenge stereotypes through the imagery, for example – such as female construction workers, male beauty therapists, and same-sex family combinations? As an educator, the responsibility to reflect the world as it is sits very much with us, but also there are people in your class who will find validation in the fact you recognise the world and its peoples have moved on.*

You'll have noticed in the observation criteria, there is direct reference to how you as the teacher are promoting equality and diversity, and through your use of resources is a very easy way to do this. Whether this is embedded within your overall delivery (again, images can easily be a part of your presentation slides, as well as your specific resources for that session).

In addition to this, you can use some of the images to prompt a discussion (if it is relevant and appropriate to do so) about changing roles etc within the world. Similarly, your use of images may stimulate less enlightened comments from some learners, which gives you the opportunity to challenge these ideas with reason and modern thinking, and pull the other learners into a brief but essential classroom conversation about the merits or otherwise of the point raised.

Yes, I did call it essential. Under our duty of care, not least when considering the Equality Act (2010) and the Counter-Terrorism & Security Act (2015), which is concerned with issues of radicalisation, we need to openly tackle and challenge any views that could be interpreted as discriminatory. Discrimination is illegal. You are the face of your organisation in that session, and you may have no way of knowing how someone in that room may be negatively affected by someone making ignorant comments, however humourously intended. As the face of the organisation you have no option – you need to tackle this square on. If this is difficult for you, them seek guidance from your line manager, but do not ignore it.

You do not, of course, have to produce all your resources yourself. The beauty of accessing online resources can mean you spend less time creating stuff from scratch. However, this may be offset by the amount of time you have to look for stuff online. Video posting sites are usually quite good, especially if you are looking for specific keywords (the main features of the video you are after). The intelligent use of video clips shouldn't be underestimated, as it can help bring the outside world into the learning environment, and can provide a lot of very useful insights. A cautionary note, however – the use of videos should never become a substitute for actual delivery. Again, they are a resource and not a method, so use them wisely to move learning forwards.

> **REALITY CHECK:**
>
> *You may rely upon a range of resources, such as textbooks or tablets, for example, but can you look at other possibilities?*
>
> (i) *Look at the topic of your next session and the activities you are already considering using*
>
> (ii) *What resources are you planning to use, and do they really put the learning in the hands of your learners? Could you introduce an alternative resource or set of resources to better support the learners in taking a more active role in pursuing their own learning?*

Making communication count

The role of communication in the learning environment is paramount. Without effective communication, learning is doomed from the start. This is no over-dramatisation; communication is key.

Don't forget, effective communication is an ongoing process. The simple act of speaking, or writing, the intended message you want your learners to receive is not in itself effective communication. Indeed, the communication is only truly effective once the message has been received and understood (in the way it was intended).

Communication takes many forms, whether it is the verbal communication between the teacher and the learners, or indeed learners and learners, or picking up on non-verbal cues. Let's not also forget the amount of written communication we can depend upon when interacting with learners. Much has been written on communication, and in much more detail than we can afford it in these pages, so some personal research might be in order. That said, communication is the lifeblood of effective teaching and learning, so let's break this down.

Verbal communication – the most obvious form of communication and often the most easily hampered. Clarity of message, or instruction, is vitally important. Never assume that what you mean is obvious; remember your audience, they are not as certain or as knowledgeable in the topics as you are, so ensure you watch your directions for how they may be open to misinterpretation. Getting learners to clarify their understanding through different techniques is a useful way of closing this particular circuit.

A word of advice – avoid asking learners if 'they understand' what you have requested of them; consider the psychology – if they haven't understood, they may feel like the problem is them, thus making them reluctant to admit this openly. Worse, they may believe they *do* understand, whilst they actually don't. Either way, you're unlikely to get a meaningful response. A better approach it to take the responsibility of clarity onto your own shoulders, and ask if what you have requested 'makes sense' as, if it doesn't, you may not have been clear enough. Often learners will respond more positively to this, and you get to ensure they have grasped what you are expecting.

Non-verbal communication (including body language) – somewhat more subtle, non-verbal communication can still have its issues. Being mindful of how you present yourself in terms of your tone, as well as your stance (including how well you respect your learners' personal space) is every bit as vital as what you say.

Consider how you stand when addressing the group. Do you present as open to their thoughts and ideas, or are you closed off and reluctant to engage with them on a human level? Do you communicate equally with all? It is an old adage that teachers don't have favourites, but despite how some choose to behave, teachers are humans too. We can develop fondness for some and adopt less favourable views of others. It's only natural, and indeed not every learner will like you as their teacher. Human nature to one side, what is essential is that your professional behaviours dominate your emotional ones and you don't demonstrate these feelings – positive or negative. Not only can it undermine your own position but it can make learners also feel uncomfortable.

Written communication – a real mainstay in how we interact with our learners, written communication is often an area within observations where teachers fall down. Why? Usually due to a lack of attention to detail, be it spelling or grammar in presentation slides, or even within handouts issued to the learners to augment their learning. With a national agenda to improve the overall standards of English and mathematics skills in the populace, teachers are bastions of the language, and attention to correct spelling and grammar is essential. Think how it looks to learners when their own teacher doesn't care enough to ensure they have spelt correctly. It doesn't say much for the standards of the organisation, or the ability of their teacher to mark their work effectively either! Basically – poor spelling and grammar from a teacher? No excuse.

Affirmative and active listening – the flip side of all this communication business; listening to our learners – not just listening to reply, but really listening to understand them. Learners need to feel valued and indeed a valuable part of the learning group. This can be achieved by the teacher engendering an atmosphere conducive to mutual support and respect, and lying at the heart of this is listening. True attentiveness to what learners are telling us is so important. Not only can it help us to meet their individual needs, but it can inform our planning as well. It can help us plan our seating arrangement, not to mention the pace we work at. If we don't listen to our learners then our communication skills are incomplete, and we probably aren't providing them with the level of service they have the right to expect.

Common communication problems
There are a couple of key issues frequently arising when we are communicating with our learners that manifest in observations, so it is important to tackle these head on.

Firstly – teachers, especially inexperienced teachers, can fall into the trap of thinking that, as the teacher, they need to be the one who speaks the most in the room. At times, that may be true, but overall the more active participation the learners are engaged in, the better their learning experience overall. Teachers need to be brave enough to step back and let learners learn. Yes, of course you need to set the activities and put the wheels for learning in motion, but then, once that is done, great – now let the magic happen. Let them work without the teacher butting in to see how it's going. Over-teaching is a real concern within the profession and can potentially smother learning opportunities, especially if we are encouraging independence.

Obviously, this is not to say the teacher role is redundant, but there is a balance to be struck here. Too much teacher-centrality is not useful when developing autonomous and free thinking learners, so really look at your planned delivery. Are you spending more time leading the session than letting the learners actively participate? Of course they need to have your input, and indeed you are still planning and facilitating the learning activities even if you are hovering in the background, but learners can retain much more when they have been actively involved in securing that knowledge for themselves.
Perhaps you can introduce rules for an activity; each group can

ask a maximum of two questions of you during the task, and any other problems they need to resolve themselves (or trading answers/ideas with neighbouring groups in their class). Alternatively, you can provide each group with a set of written instructions to follow, so that the dynamic of the task is very different, but those instructions must be clear, and unambiguous.

Too much teacher talk is by far the most common communication problem seen during classroom observations. Teachers feel they need to show off their skills, or their knowledge, sadly at the expense of the learners' experience. Communication is most effective when it is concise and clear. Don't flood the room with too much – the learners may not cope well, and will start to suffer from information saturation. Once you reach that point, communication is breaking down and you won't get the results you're after anyway.

The other key problem is one mentioned briefly before – a lack of attention to detail. Where communication is verbal or written, the clarity is essential. Remember, as teachers we know what we are talking about (more often than not, anyway), but the learners may not. We need to monitor our speech and our written instructions to ensure we don't make assumptions about prior knowledge, and to eliminate ambiguity.

Ambiguity is a real problem for learners, no matter how old they are. If instructions are open to interpretation, this can lead to disaster for an activity, and getting things wrong can, for many learners, be a demotivating outcome. It may be that in some cases, you welcome learners interpreting tasks how they wish, especially if this nurtures creativity, but if there is a clear intention that needs to be adhered to, then ensure the instruction is completely clear. Don't ask yourself 'can I understand this?' when reflecting, ask yourself 'how could this be misunderstood?' instead, and you might surprise yourself with what you find.

Barriers to effective communication

There are a range of factors that can impact on effective communication with your learners, and whilst you will undoubtedly be covering communication and communication theories on your course, when it comes to your observed assessments, it is worth considering what factors can impact on the effective communication taking place in the session.

It's useful to consider both internal and external factors that can detrimentally affect communication. Please be aware these lists are not exhaustive, and you will benefit from being open to recognising a range of wider factors.

Internal factors – these can originate from within the learners themselves, and can be hard to manage other than through sensitivity, empathy and patience. Internal factors negatively impacting on effective communication can include English as an additional language; visual or hearing impairments; low self-esteem and belief in own ability; historical behaviourial conditions such as ADHD; dyslexia (which can also effect the ability to process and retain a series of linear instructions) along with others.

External factors – these are usually more environmental in nature, but can include noise (inside or outside the classroom); the temperature of the space they are in; other learners (who can be distracting); information overload (too much to process at once); or any aspect that may generate stress, such as impending tests, for example.

There are many things that can impede effective communication, so ensuring that you, as the teacher, are the solution and not part of the problem is vital. General awareness of what is occurring within your learning environment needs to be maintained, so you can take action to eliminate such factors where you can. Otherwise, simply ensuring your intention is received through meaningful checking is a core responsibility of the teacher. If a learner has failed to understand, it probably isn't their fault; it will be ours for not successfully checking we made ourselves fully understood.

> **REALITY CHECK:**
>
> *Without effective communication, your sessions are unlikely to be successful for your learners.*
>
> *Consider the layout of your learning environment (it may help to draw it out) – where do you normally position yourself? Can all the learners see and hear you clearly at all points? Do you move around? Does that disadvantage anyone? Can learners all see and hear each other to facilitate maximum engagement?*
>
> *As an experiment, map out the lines of communication as they take place, using arrows to demonstrate the direction of travel of the various messages passing around in the room. Remember – it isn't always verbal!*

Reflection in action: your flexible friend

The last section of this chapter considers that valuable tool in the teacher's toolkit – reflection. The ability to reflect allows you, as a professional practitioner, to critically consider the work you have undertaken with an analytical eye; this enables you to not only recognise the work that has been most effective (in terms of activities, learner responsiveness, pace etc) but also where things (i) didn't go as well as anticipated and (ii) how to improve delivery for the future.

The future is an important feature of reflection – because you can't change the past. People sometimes feel that reflecting on their delivery can help them re-write history, and ensure when delivering that session again it will be better.

You will never deliver that session again!

That may seem an odd thing to say, but even if the intention is to deliver the same course time after time, that session you just delivered has gone. You'll never deliver it to those learners again, and so their dynamic will never impact on the overall structure, pace, discussions and points arising ever again. You can't change it. But you can learn from it.

Effective reflection accepts that you cannot drag and drop the experiences from one session with one cohort to another. It also recognises that you have the opportunity to grow professionally as a result of the experience so you are better equipped when confronted by similar occurrences. Yes, there may be some minor technical tweaks you can make to the session, having reflected on it but, more importantly, you'll have identified behavioural triggers that occur that you can avoid, not just when you reach this point again next time you deliver the course, but also in future sessions (irrespective of topic).

Much has been written over the years on the use of reflection, and your course will probably steer you towards the writings of Schon on 'the reflective practitioner' (or how professionals think in action). Whilst he produced several works, his 1983 and 1987 books (*'The Reflective Practitioner'* and *'Educating the Reflective Practitioner'* respectively) generated a lot of discussion around two strands of active reflective process, namely reflecting on action, and reflecting in action.

Reflecting on action is a concept the follows the general model of reflective practice, namely that the teacher reviews, critically, their preceding performance (including all of the component aspects, such as learners, time management, range and suitability of activities and so forth) with a view to identify their strengths and also any areas for development that can be extrapolated and tackled for any and all future delivery. Part of the teacher's responsibility as a member of their educational community is to be a part of the process for continuous quality improvement, and this self-reflective activity building on the often simple evaluation of their sessions, is so very important.

Reflection in action is a slightly different approach to this, and requires the professional not to wait until after the event, but actually to be sufficiently critically aware in the moment of what is happening to be able to effect change as required to resolve issues or problems as they develop. Sounds complex? Well, it both is and isn't (helpfully).

The thought processes involved in effective reflection in action are rapid, and solutions focused. This means that the practitioner has spotted that something isn't working, or is beginning not to work, either for the class, or for individuals, and needs to be resolved. The identification of a resolution is both instinctive and intellectually driven, and results in an alternative plan being implemented to salvage the emerging situation.

This is unlikely to happen to dramatic extents in every session – or at least, it shouldn't, not least if you are reflecting on action regularly. However, it may on occasion happen on a grand scale, where whole activities need to be reshaped or abandoned in favour of a different approach, for example. More likely it will happen in small ways; you'll spot learners aren't quite 'getting it' or one or two can't quite engage with the task. What do you do? Well, the best kind of teacher will demonstrate a degree of responsive flexibility and take steps to adjust (on a minor or major scale) the aspect of the session that – for whatever reason – isn't working. It won't be in the session plan, for obvious reasons, but it will be something you will want to signify to your observer, as responding flexibly to meet individual need is a criterion, and if you are doing it seamlessly, they may need a nudge to spot it!

I say it won't be in your session plan, but could it be? In some cases, you may anticipate that not all learners will be able to engage with specific tasks, and so you have differentiated for them suitably to ensure appropriate levels of stretch and challenge are applied throughout. But perhaps you have also considered, as part of your planning for individual need, that they may achieve more quickly than anticipated and so you have a back-up plan for that eventuality. This is arguably also you being flexible in your delivery, as you have built in the opportunity to be additionally responsive to need.

REALITY CHECK:

Reflecting in action is often an instinctive act for teachers, responding as they do to situations as they naturally arise.

- *(i) Take a moment of introspection: can you look back on previous teaching session and identify where you have proactively made in-class changes to the plan as a result of spotting 'issues'?*

- *(ii) Putting yourself in the place of an observer, how would you have spotted this? Could you as the teacher do something to ensure the observer recognises this flexibility?*

Now read through the following and consider the points arising:

Case Study: Alan & Mike's Team-Taught Art & Animation Media Class

Alan and Mike work together to deliver this Extended National Diploma Level 3 qualification for 16 learners wishing to access the video games manufacturing and design industry. It is also a useful way of teaching coding and digital animation skills, but the course also requires wider skills such as pitching a game concept, and designing the marketing, for example.

This session is focusing on developing the marketing strategy and is led by Mike. Alan is also in the room, having provided some catch-up support to a learner, Samilla, who missed the last lesson. Mike has established an activity whereby the learners need to use their desktop computers to investigate existing, leading game marketing campaigns, and evaluate how effective they are for a class presentation to feedback in 25 minutes. However, Alan has noticed that a few of the learners are just looking up 'marketing strategies' and others are more focused on checking out the latest games on the market. Mike picked up on this too, and in trying to bring the learners back on task, has asked that instead of working independently they now pair-up with the learner next to them so they can share findings and so present back together.

This resulted in an increase in the in-class chatter, and even more distance from the task. Alan offers to take on half the class if Mike wants to change the activity, so that they can form two separate groups looking at the effectiveness of current market strategies, with a specific game in mind for each team, so that it becomes a group-based activity rather than pair work to try to manage it better. Mike likes the idea, but worries it's a bit late in the activity to change it again, especially as the clock is ticking. At this point, Samilla says that she can't keep up with the pair work as she is still trying to complete the urgent task from the last session, and asks Mike which thing he wants her to concentrate on.

When working with a large class, it can be useful to build in some personal research into the session to empower and involve the learners directly in what they are learning, but sometimes distractions can creep in, even if the level is quite demanding.

Consider the following questions in relation to Alan and Mike's session, and let's see what you would do:

1. *The initial concept is a good one, but perhaps Mike could have anticipated the potential for the learners to go off-task – what could he have done differently from the start to more effectively manage the situation, to keep learners focused?*
2. *Alan's suggestion of creating two teams to work collaboratively on a specific marketing campaign each is also not a bad idea. Taking Mike's concerns into account, would you have implemented this, and if so, how? If not – why?*
3. *Samilla missed the last session and is trying to catch-up in class. Perhaps this is because she hasn't got access to specific software, or hardware, etc at home. Whatever the reason, her need to complete it is another factor impacting negatively on the task, as she can't participate as a pair. What could Mike and Alan do about this, to keep learning moving forwards for everyone?*
4. *This allows us to consider some in-class flexibility, but if we go a step further and reflect on action, and had to revisit this session – what might we put in place differently to support the learners in the task of investigating and evaluating existing marketing strategies for recently released games from the start? You can consider the range of approaches that are available to you.*

It can be very easy to see what is wrong with someone else's session, and not so easy to see what is going badly in our own. Developing this reflective practice is very important to a teacher's development, as there won't always be an observer in the room to provide us with feedback to help us to recognise these stumbles. We need to feel comfortable enough with our own professionalism to accept things won't always go as well as we plan for them to, and learn from it. Burying our heads is not a workable solution, and we can always do something better, and find something to learn from.

In Alan and Mike's case, it would have been fine to move the footing to two groups, as it is almost a progressive task. Firstly, individual work is completed, and then it is shared in pairs. Next – taking Alan's idea forwards – those pairs are teamed up, with a view to focusing on one of the marketing strategies they have found per group. This could be a decision voted on by the group members from the work undertaken. If they haven't contributed sufficiently, then they can't be disappointed with the choice made. It keeps the dynamic moving, and would also then allow for individuals within the larger groups to have roles to fulfill in the completion of the task.

Samilla could be told to focus on this task now, and arrangements made to catch up after the session. Otherwise, she runs the risk of being behind on two tasks instead of just one. What is important to consider here is both the impact on the learner, and where the priority lies. Clearly, keeping her on track is essential so the current task needs to be her focus. Perhaps Alan could have made that clearer from the start.

There are numerous alternative options also available, and no doubt you'll have come up with several. There is no 'one true way' to plot out a series of activites and a multitude of alternative avenues to pursue if things start to go in a direction other than the intended one. Keeping calm, remaining outcome and learner focused, you will see what needs to be tweaked and make the necessary adjustments. Sometimes it's just okay to say: "well that's not working, is it? Let's try something different" and no respect will be diminished in doing so.

Being flexible in our classes is something we do automatically. Admittedly, early in teaching careers, new and freshly minted trainees feel compelled to hold on fast to the structure and order that the lesson plan provides, which is entirely understandable, as they aren't bad comfort blankets. But experience will teach you – possibly far better than it can be articulated here – that even the most meticulously planned session can be subjected to the most unexpected element of all – the learners.

What they ask, how they react, how well they receive an activity you have selected to use – you think you can predict it (and mostly you will be right) – but there will always be the curve ball, straight out of left field that you didn't quite expect. But you don't panic, or run; you try to catch the ball. You might drop it, for the slightest of moments, but then you pick it up before anyone really notices. Then you adapt. You see what needs changing and you do it. For most teachers, this is instinctive. Up to this point, you've probably never given it a thought, but as you were asked in the last Reality Check point, looking back you'll probably see you bend and flex to ensure the smooth running of your sessions far more regularly than you make a mental note of.

All I'm asking of you now is to make, at least for the duration of your teacher-training course (by which point it will become second nature), the conscious effort to make that mental note when you made an in-class adaptation to respond to the changing circumstances or the learners' needs. Take that mental note and annotate it when you evaluate your lesson. Recognise these additional skills you possess that help you deliver the best lessons you can. Don't let these small, but vital, demonstrations of your flexibility get lost in the business of teaching – they are part of its heart.

This chapter has considered all of the mandatory criteria that pertains to the delivery of learning, ranging from the selection of the teaching and learning approaches you're adopting, the resources you're using (and how you might be promoting equality and diversity through their use and in general). We have also considered how you communicate effectively with learners, and can be flexible in your delivery, as need demands. Basically, we've covered a lot.

The next chapter considers the application of assessment within your teaching and learning sessions, and will explore how you use it to inform your own monitoring of progress, as well as your planning. We'll also consider some of the more challenging elements that trainees face when trying to evidence what they have done to their observers.

5 ASSESSMENT: MONITORING, TRACKING & USING

This chapter will explore ways in which the teacher monitors how effectively new learning has taking place, and will consider the role of assessment for learning, of learning and as learning; furthermore, we will look at the range of suitable assessment instruments, and how well they support the principles of assessment. In addition, the notion of measuring progress and achievement will be considered, and how this can be supported by well constructed learning objectives and outcomes for any given session.

This chapter relates to the following Professional Standards:

Professional values and attributes – (1) Evaluate what works best in your teaching and learning to meet the diverse needs of your learners; (2) Evaluate and challenge your practice, values and beliefs; (3) Inspire, motivate and raise expectations for learners through your enthusiasm and knowledge; (4) Be creative and innovative in selecting and adapting strategies to help learners to learn; (5) Value and promote social and cultural diversity, equality of opportunity and inclusion; (6) Build positive and collaborative relationships with colleagues and learners

Professional knowledge and understanding *– (7) Maintain and update knowledge of your subject and/or vocational area; (9) Apply theoretical understanding of effective practice in teaching, learning and assessment drawing on research and other evidence; (10) Evaluate your practice with others to assess its impact on learning; (11); Manage and promote positive learner behaviour; (12) Understand the teaching and professional role and your responsibilities*

Professional skills *– (13) Motivate and inspire learners to promote achievement and develop their skills to enable progression; (14) Plan and deliver effective learning programmes for diverse groups; (15) Promote the benefits of technology and support learners in its use; (16) Address the mathematics and English needs of learners, and work creatively to overcome individual barriers to learning; (17) Enable learners to share responsibility for their own learning and assessment, setting goals that stretch and challenge; (18) Apply appropriate and fair methods of assessment and provide constructive and timely feedback to support progression and achievement; (20) Contribute to organisational development and quality improvement through collaboration with others*

The development of new learning is a core value of our work. Of course it is, but we need to know that learning has not only taken place, but clear attainment has occurred. It is great that our learners experience their new learning, through your well planned and executed learning sessions, but can they apply this new learning as they move forwards?

As a teacher, remember you are striving to equip your learners to develop their skills, knowledge and competency in your subject so that they can, ultimately, operate independently of you. A scary thought, perhaps, but really that's an underpinning reason for them attending your sessions – to acquire all that they need so that they can move on without you. Don't take it personally, it's what you're there for. In fact, them achieving this autonomy is a tribute to your own skills as a teacher, so there's a bright side for you, too. But before this emergence into independence you first need to be confident that they have learned all they were required to, and this is where assessment comes in to play.

Assessment has may forms, many means and many functions. It serves many masters in modern-day education, but its foundation remains solid – it is there for you to check and track your learners' progress and achievements. As such, there is a lot to demonstrate to your assessing observer(s) in relation to this.

Let's look at the criteria from your observations that relates to assessment that we'll be exploring in this chapter:

1. *Confirm how the candidate has communicated with other learning professionals to meet individual needs and encourage progression*
2. *Confirm how the candidate has used types and methods of assessment, including peer and self assessment, to (a) involve learners in assessment, (b) meet individual needs of learners, (c) enable learners to produce assessment evidence that is reliable, sufficient, authentic and current, (d) meet internal and external assessment requirements*
3. *Confirm how the candidate has applied minimum core elements in planning, delivering and assessing*
4. *Confirm how the candidate has demonstrated flexibility and adaptability in using types and methods of assessment to meet individual requirements and assessment requirements*
5. *Confirm how the candidate has used assessment data in (a) monitoring learners' achievement, attainment and progress, (b) setting learners' targets, (c) planning subsequent sessions, and (d) recording the outcome of assessment*

Like I said, there's a lot to cover. Luckily, some of the work overlaps neatly, so if you're taking care of one aspect, you'll be picking up a couple of other aspects too. This will become clearer as we work through this chapter. Much like facing an assessment itself, don't become fazed by the criteria – there is nothing stipulated in there that a decent teacher wouldn't already be applying, or starting to apply, to their regular practice. Interweaving assessment of learning through your natural cycle of planning, delivery and evaluation will become second nature, if it isn't already. But let's kick off with one of the tricky bits – the language of assessment.

Talking 'types': categorising the phases of assessment

As we have seen, all professions have their own jargon, or technical language associated with it, and education is no different in this respect. Earlier, in Chapter Two, we looked at the 'principles of assessment' (*validity, authenticity, reliability, sufficiency, and currency*) which all have specific meanings in relation to assessment, and the suitability of the instruments (or approaches) we elect to use.

Another piece of the educational jargon we need to get to grips with is the difference between assessment and evaluation. Certainly, in the outside world, the terms are interchangeable but within education, this is not the case. For us, assessment is a measure of learning, however we enact it, and evaluation is a reflective process by which we determine how effective something has been. That something could include an activity or an entire session. Ultimately it could be a course (and we may even want to seek evaluative feedback from our learners to use to support our own evaluation). But do be mindful when talking about evaluating, we are not talking about assessing and vice versa.

Similarly – and this may well start to sound increasingly nit-picky, so if you have your educational glossary that you're creating close by, it may be time to go into overdrive! – but we need to clear up the differences between types and methods of assessing.

Types (or phases) of assessment: These are usually broken down into three categories – initial, formative and summative. Important to lead with here is that types are not methods in their own right. They are timeframes in the teaching, learning and assessment cycle during which point aspects of learning are being checked. Let us consider this in a little more detail:

- **Initial assessment** – undertaken at the start of a course, or possibly prior to the start of the course. Primarily used to determine existing levels of ability, including knowledge and skills, as well as – ideally – the learners' motivation, learning preferences (if you feel it will help), and what they wish to achieve. Initial assessment is often associated with the term 'diagnostic assessment' which, again is in the initial stages of the process, but is more focused on specific functional skills levels (English and maths, usually). Initial assessment should be used to inform session planning, as it will help you to determine how best to group or pair up your learners, and indeed how best to differentiate to ensure maximum stretch and challenge at all times.
- **Formative assessment** – an on-going process throughout the learning journey, formative assessment is often also referred to as *Assessment for Learning (AfL)*, which you may have heard of. The approach to formative assessment can be formal or, more frequently, it tends to be informal, with the teacher skillfully using a range of methods to elicit how well learners are attaining in class, and what new learning has been assimilated. Assessment for learning is dependent on the teacher making effective use of feedback to ensure that (i) learners are aware of their own

progress and achievements, but also (ii) to ensure that they know what is required of them to improve. This information should also be tracked by the teacher so to inform future planning, as well as allow at-a-glance reviews of individual progress.

- **Summative assessment** – also known as *Assessment of Learning (AoL)*, summative assessment takes place at points of completion on courses. By this, I mean the end of a topic, or of a unit, or ultimately the end of the course. Usually formal in approach, the Assessment of Learning is the point at which teachers or assessors are able to confer competency, or certification, upon their learners, having ably demonstrated their ability to successfully meet the standards. This can be practically, or through testing. We will consider different methods that are available to you shortly.

An observer is going to need to see that you have effectively undertaken at least initial, and probably some formative, assessment with your learners in advance of the session they are coming to observe. The use of your assessment records will be invaluable here, and a little later in this chapter we shall explore this in more detail.

Assessment records alone, however, are not the only place the observer will seek evidence of assessment – the goals you established that we discussed in Chapter 3 will, in part at least, be linked to your initial assessment of your learners, to establish their reasons for being on the course (their motivation, if you like), and their intentions for using the course in the future (is it to access a higher level course, or to develop specific skills to advance in employment, for example?).

Read the following case study, then let's consider the points below:

Case Study: Marty's First Observation

Marty delivers Employability Skills courses, run in conjunction with the local JobCentre Plus (JCP). Marty has her learners sent to her via the JCP's advisors, who book their clients onto her course at the local FE College. Marty delivers a course that attracts funding, but not much, so the college has set the course up to be run over three consecutive days. She meets them for the first time on Day 1. The course covers a range of skills, such as CV writing, online job searching, composing cover letters, interview technique as well as providing softer outcomes, such as confidence to speak in public, personal presentation and so on. There are a couple of accredited units attached to the course, so the learners complete worksheets to evidence their ability and achievement.

The course is 'off-the-shelf' so has little scope in the short time provided to allow for significant differentiation of content, and sadly many of the learners have had poor 'work-training' experiences prior to this course at the hands of other providers. Marty is a dedicated teacher and wants to ensure the course works well for all those attending, and has a meaningful impact.

Marty's observer has come to see her on the second session of one of these courses, and upon arrival asked for her teaching folder, on the assumption that any assessment records will be included within it. Marty explains the set-up of the course is atypical of other courses she delivers, and scope for assessment outside of the criteria for achieving the accreditations is extremely limited.

The observer's report noted that whilst there was good formative assessment through questioning and the set activities, Marty had not made effective use of initial assessment to allow for any individualisation or contextualisation of the learning, or to inform her planning in general. Similarly, the observer was concerned that without starting points recorded, authentic progress was hard to evidence, calling into question the summative outcomes.

Don't worry – the rest of the report was fine! Marty, however, clearly does need to give some thought to how she can undertake some sort of initial assessment in what is clearly a very short space of time available to her.

Have a think about the following:

1. Marty clearly has limited time on the course to include any large type of initial assessment activity, so what options would you encourage her to consider to work around this?
2. Formative assessment is working well, with informal questioning techniques being used to check learning – is this something you would consider (a) factoring into your lesson plan, or would it be ad hoc, and (b) would you be able to use any initial assessment information to plan your questioning techniques to be even better? How?
3. What on earth is the observer talking about when making that point about the authenticity of the outcomes? Is it something Marty needs to worry about?

There are a lot of courses being developed nationally to respond to emerging priorities, and employability sits well in this category; these are often short courses, which work best for the client group, and certainly are very much pre-developed for a quick turnaround. However, even though these courses are developed to meet a national need, the level of professionalism demonstrated of the teaching staff remains the same, as without such things as an initial assessment, then Marty's course may also get the same bad reputation as those less successful training courses the clients had been sent to. Why? Because they were probably faceless, impersonal skills factories, focused on outputs rather than the impact on the learners. Luckily for Marty's learners, she cares enough to take the observer's points on board.

It can be hard to fit in an initial assessment to a tightly planned course, but it is essential if you want to make it viable. Perhaps something as simple as getting learners to introduce themselves and answering three or four specific questions when doing so will allow you enough of an initial insight to start making your own observations about the people you have, their needs, strengths and where they may struggle. It may even be worth taking notes you can then write up into an initial assessment record, so at least you can reflect on this when planning small group or pair work. Yes, it is a snapshot but you might not have a lot of time to play with. On longer courses, you'd of course undertake a much more meaningful initial assessment, probably over a couple of sessions, to get a fuller picture.

What is important to remember with an initial assessment is that point about it being a snapshot. It is a point early on in their journey with you, and it won't be who they are for very long. So it is worth revisiting it along the way, and updating it as skills grow and develop, and as goals shift and change.

Indeed, having this understanding of who is strong with what can absolutely help you frame your informal questioning of learners; by knowing the levels of ability in your group, you can differentiate the level of complexity required of answers, and target individuals you know will be suitably challenged to answer, but with minimal risk of them failing. This also builds confidence. Using nominated questions (where you, as the teacher, nominate the person you wish to answer) allows for this, and also ensures you are drawing all your learners into the session. Recording this on your lesson plan is an excellent idea, as it acts as an aide memoir for you, and also demonstrates to an observer the extent of your planning for both differentiation and formative assessment. Two birds with one stone – can't be bad!

The last point Marty had to worry about was this question of authenticity, which is one of the principles of assessment. What the observer was getting at is the fact that without the learners' starting points recorded (by which we mean their skills/ability/knowledge etc. at the point of joining the course) then how can we be sure that their progress towards completing the qualification (or whatever) is legitimate? How do we know they weren't already able to complete the criteria? As such, can we be sure that learning has actually taken place at all, or have they merely been coasting through?

This is applicable to any course, whether there is an accreditation attached or not – as the teacher, you need to be confidently demonstrating that from the point at which those learners started their course, new learning has taken place. Shortly, we will look at how you could record that, but first we need to consider the methods available to you so that you can complete the assessments in the first place.

To test, or not to test: exploring assessment instruments

How to assess is every bit as important as what you are assessing and, as with teaching methods, not every approach to assessing will best suit every assessment requirement. Where the assessments are part of a formal, externally accredited qualification, there may be prescribed methods of assessment, but often these can be left to the discretion and professional judgment of the teacher designing and delivering the course.

On non-accredited courses, the teacher has much more freedom; not only are you developing your own criteria, but the approaches you adopt to assess them are (usually) completely your own choice. As with session planning, it would take a separate publication to cover all the nuances of assessment, and indeed several publications focusing on this are readily available. Here, we need to consider what your observer is looking for and how to ensure you are meeting the standards of your own qualification.

Assessment methods, or instruments as they can often be more officiously referred to, take many shapes and forms. We have mentioned questioning already, but there are is a wealth of alternatives. Consider the simple quiz, or a crossword; perhaps a timed practical activity? Maybe you need to deploy a role-play to allow your learners to demonstrate their skills and knowledge. Perhaps learners have to produce essays, or even complete an end of course exam.

Remember what assessment is being used for – you need to be clear on this to inform what methods you are best placed to select to meet both the needs of the course, but also the needs of your learners. It is a common misconception that certain assessment activities can only be used for initial assessment or formative assessment purposes, for example, but I would challenge this. After all, many assessment methods can be used during any of those phases, as long as they suit the reason you are assessing. In many ways, an activity you complete for an initial assessment may be extremely useful as a formative OR summative assessment if repeated later, if it allows you a very clear and authentic representation of the distance travelled by that learner.

Of course, some instruments are better suited for more formal, summative assessments (exams spring directly to mind here), but again, you can use your professional judgment and be innovative. Remember the principles of assessment discussed earlier? If in doubt about how effective an assessment method is, consider evaluating it using those principles; does it provide authentic evidence? How do you know? Is it reliable? Does its use give you sufficient evidence to make an informed decision on how well learning has been attained? There is no magic formula for this, sadly; it will come with experience and reflection (and possibly the occasional misstep, too), but that's fine, mistakes are there for all of us to learn from. It won't, of course, hurt to start building up some of this reflection now, as it will undoubtedly help and support you in your growing work as a teacher.

On the following page there is a grid for you to complete, in which I've listed a few assessment methods for you to reflect on. Also, within the grid, is space for you to collect your thoughts on whether the method is better suited for the initial, formative or summative phase of assessment, and what its strengths and limitations are as an approach. It may help to copy the grid onto an A4 sheet, to allow you to make your own notes.

When considering the strengths and the limitations, draw on the principles of assessment as mentioned above. Use them as a critical lens through which you can identify if, as a method, it does allow your learners the opportunity to produce evidence that is authentic, sufficient, reliable and so forth. Remember, what for you constitutes authenticity in a learner's work? That it is their own work? Yes, but how do you *know* that for sure? Are you confident the assessment tool used provides this opportunity? If it does, great, if it doesn't, then that may well be a limitation, but it doesn't automatically mean you wouldn't use it; you may simply use it as part of a wider assessment strategy for the course as a whole.

When considering limitations, consider also the needs of learners – there may well be some assessment tools that are very rigid (by necessity) but if learners have additional needs, then does that impact on how fair the assessment is for them? Or may it bring back memories of prior bad experiences in the school system? Can we be sensitive to this?

You may also see a couple of terms you are unfamiliar with – that's no bad thing; you may well wish to go away and research them a little, possibly even with the added value that you'll end up using something new to enhance your own delivery and assessment.

Assessment Reflective Analysis

	Initial/Formative/Summative?	Strengths	Limitations
Quiz			
Essay (Homework)			
Simulation (Role-Play)			
Case Study			
Self-Assessment			
Peer-Assessment			
Exam			
Question & Answer			

Hopefully, you'll be able to see from completing the grid that all of the assessment methods have some validity when it comes to their use, you just need to be confident in using them. Remember – when you are being observed, your assessor will be looking for your use of assessment methods that will deliver the type of evidence you need to check learning has taken place, and new learning has been attained.

You'll have noticed that the grid made direct reference to peer and self-assessment as well. These can be extremely useful approaches for involving your learners in the assessment process, but you do need to manage them effectively. Let us quickly reflect on what we need to take into consideration when we adopt peer and self-assessment activities.

Self-Assessment – this places the onus on the learners to judge their own level of ability and learning (prior or new). This is a useful reflective tool, and can also be used well, in conjunction with a teacher's own assessment, to provide an insight into the learner. After all, learners often have inaccurate or incomplete views of their own skills-level; these can range for greatly underplaying their abilities to grossly overstating them! Self-assessment is often over-used as a quick-fix initial assessment approach but, sadly, without the teacher following this up themselves. As a result, a cautionary note would be that self-assessment in isolation has the potential to be unreliable, if the teacher is using it specifically to capture starting points, for example, but if part of a wider assessment strategy then it can give you a much better-informed bigger picture.

When you consider how to ensure self-assessment may be seen during an observation, I would suggest that any opportunity you give your learners to reflect on how well they accomplished a task, what they think they could have done better or differently in future, allows you to state in your session plan that some degree of self-assessment has been planned for.

Peer-Assessment – a much under-utilised approach that really can support assessment for learning, whilst involving learners in the process of assessment. Of course, those participating need to have a clear understanding of what they are actually assessing, and be able to provide some form of meaningful feedback. The use of peers works best when it is structured, so possibly the provision of a teacher-developed peer feedback form would help support this, funneling the learners' attention to specific points. The down side to peers undertaking assessment can be bias and a lack of skills when it comes to being effectively critical and providing meaningfully constructive feedback. As mentioned, this approach has a lot of potential to work well, but it does need to be effectively managed (and yes, that does mean planned).

Don't forget that your observer needs to see you using peer and self-assessment techniques across the sessions they observe you delivering and so, whilst these may quite legitimately not be a feature of every session you deliver, you know from the off they need to be a feature in some of them. Perhaps you can use these observations as an opportunity to experiment with peer and self-assessment activities so that the observer can give you some feedback – after all, don't forget that your assessor's role is to provide developmental feedback too.

> ***REALITY CHECK:***
>
> *Consider your last session, and your next one. What assessment methods did you, and are you planning to use? Are they clearly defined in your session plans?*
>
> *Is there scope to incorporate – however informally – peer or self-assessment in the next session? Could it add value to an activity, and also promote assessment for learning?*

Accessing fair assessment: what you know, and who you know

Teachers, especially (but not exclusively) new and inexperienced teachers, often overlook the fact that the promotion of equality of opportunity also extends to the assessment of their learners too. The need for 'fair' assessment is an imperative for awarding organisations and examination boards, and most will publish guidelines on how to access fair assessment. However, fair assessment is the right of all learners, whether on accredited courses or not.

Key to this is communication. Teachers need to identify if learners have any additional learning needs that could impact on their ability to participate not only in class, but also in any assessment of their learning. How might you discover this? Certainly, if you completed any pre-course interviews, or any initial assessments, then this should have been disclosed by the learner (it is their responsibility to let you, or the organisation, know so that support can be provided). That said, late declarations are not unusual, as often people don't want to be seen as being 'a problem' or causing trouble, so you need to remain open to the possibility you may find out later than is ideal that there are support needs.

As soon as you are aware, you need to communicate this. But to whom? In all honesty, this will vary from organisation to organisation, but what is important is that you find out what is expected within your place of work, so that you can apply the local procedures and policies.

In general terms, communication should be with any number of other learning professionals to ensure that needs are met. The job titles may vary, as may the responsibilities, but here are some people you may need to liaise with:

1. **Curriculum manager.** Have you notified them of the specific needs of your learners, and can they provide any

help? They may themselves liaise directly with other professionals, or they may direct you to. Either way, keeping them up-to-date on progress, especially where you have learners where support is an issue, is good practice worth following.

2. *Inclusion Officer.* This person (or team of people) may well be able to make use of their – albeit probably limited – budget to provide material support to your learners with additional needs. This can be in the shape of specific resources, or even possibly learning support assistants (LSAs) depending on the severity and level of need disclosed.

3. *Examinations Officer.* This post holder will regularly be in touch with the awarding institutions and will be well versed in the various options available for special dispensations should learners have additional needs that could compromise the fairness of any formal assessment. They will be able to advise you on how best to prepare for that but, as a word of warning, some awarding bodies do need a lot of formal declarations very early in the process to secure legitimate and sanctioned support during formal assessments such as exams, so you will need to be on top of this.

4. *Safeguarding (& Prevent Duty) Officer.* Depending on the nature of the disclosure, you may be obliged to share information with the designated safeguarding officer. If you are uncertain about this, share the information anyway, and let them be the one to decide if they will act upon it or not. You would be well advised to familiarise yourself with the local policy on this.

5. *Learning Support Assistant.* If you do find you have a learning support assistant assigned to your class, or a

specific learner, don't forget to communicate with them, and ideally this includes not only featuring them in your session plan, but actually letting them have a copy for their own information. It is hard to be an effective support if what is expected of you is unclear!

These are just five quick examples of other educational professionals you may have to communicate with in order to ensure that you are meeting individual learners' needs. Don't forget that your assessor needs to see evidence that you have communicated with other professionals, so it may be worth keeping records of this in your teaching file. This could be email exchanges, for example, or indeed session plans demonstrating your expectations of the LSA. But make them readily available – an observer wants to watch the session, and doesn't want to spend too long poring over documentation. They need to see it, but it needs to be easily found, easily recogniseable, and easily commented on. As with an inspector, you always want to consider how best you can make the observer's job an easy one.

Developing measurable learning outcomes: making assessment meaningful

Of course, it often helps if you make your job an easier one too! As mentioned in Chapter 3, one of the most frequently recurring points for development that emerge from teacher training observations is the construction of learning outcomes that are actually measurable, and measurable in a demonstrable way.

It is a common sight to see learning outcomes that are generic for the session (so lack any degree of differentiation), but that take a vague route to define what new learning should have taken place over the duration of the session. This is such a shame, as by having really well crafted learning outcomes, it becomes much, much easier to support your formative assessment.

Consider the following learning outcome:

Learners will understand how to wire a plug.

Ok, firstly, possibly a little archaic but, as an example, let's run with it for now. Can you already spot what makes this learning outcome unhelpful from a teacher's perspective? If we wish to be really mercenary, can we also see why – from an observer's point of view – this learning outcome is somewhat flawed?

Let's consider a few other factors –

a) ***Differentiation:*** there isn't any! If we want all of our learners to be stretched and challenged throughout our sessions, then learning outcomes like this do not help us at all.
b) ***Scope for checking learning:*** how do we check 'understanding' in practical terms? Ask them? Maybe – but from experience, asking students 'if they understand?' rarely provides honest and useful responses.
c) ***Clarity around the skills/learning expected:*** do we really know from this outcome the depth of new learning and skills the teacher expects to see? I can understand how to administer CPR, for example, but does that mean I can do it?

Language is so important when constructing viable learning objectives. Often teachers cling to very narrow and limited terms that subsequently stifle them when it comes to checking learning, and indeed being able to adequately track learning.

The point around differentiation is also very significant – not all learners may be able to complete the tasks we 'expect' when they are wrapped up in something so all-encompassing, so we end up doing them – and us – a disservice. Perhaps by having differentiated learning outcomes we can (i) make it easier for us to measure individual learner's progress and achievement and (ii) allow the learners the opportunity to demonstrate their new learning more effectively. This latter point will help support an assessment strategy much more transparently too, given that the phrasing of the learning outcome can help us in determining how said outcome could be evidenced.

Let's revisit that plug!

So, considering we want to make the outcome suitable for different levels of learner in the class, let's split it up to factor that in. To make our measuring of their success in achieving these outcomes more transparent let's make our expectations less vague. Here goes…

> *All learners will be able to label the component parts of a plug, explaining what each part does, including identifying the function of the different coloured wires.*
>
> *All learners will be able to safely open a plug under supervision.*
>
> *Some learners will be able to safely disconnect one plug, and replace it with another, successfully demonstrating how to detach and re-attach the wires correctly.*
>
> *Some learners may be able to demonstrate how to remove and replace the fuse safely.*

From the original learning outcome, we now have four; two that everyone should be able to complete, one that only some will be able to complete, and one that some may be able to complete as an additional challenge. Can you see how the wording and the level of explicit detail helps with this?

Not only that, but it will also help you assess and, indeed, plan your assessment as mentioned earlier; you know you are factoring opportunities for the learners to undertake a labeling activity, which may be through an illustrated worksheet, or answering nominated questions, perhaps. You also have to allow for practical activity, and scope to allow your learners to work independently.

Of course, this is a very limited example, but as there are simply millions of potential combinations for your learning outcomes, it is not possible here to provide options for every scenario. What I can do is provide a short compendium of possible terms that may well help you frame your learning outcomes in a far more demonstrable fashion:

Define	List	Name	Label
Identify	Illustrate	Classify	Contrast
Compare	Explain	Find	Construct
Justify	Analyse	Summarise	Discuss
Determine	Present	Argue	Write

Remember - specific learning outcomes should:

- Specify precisely what the learner should know/be able to do
- Be written in such a way that it's possible to determine whether or not the objective has been achieved
- Suit the topic, the learners, and the resources available

It may well also help you to visualise what, at the end of the session, you expect your learners to be able to do that they couldn't do before it, and how exactly they are going to prove that they now can.

Let's look at the following case study, and consider the points arising afterwards. Whilst reading it, do please consider your own approaches to structuring learning outcomes in your own classes, and how you check to see they have been achieved.

Case Study: Liam's Learning Outcomes

Liam is a new teacher who has recently been appointed to start delivering an Extended National Diploma (Level 3) in Hospitality and Catering. Despite 9 years as a professional chef, Liam has only just started teaching, and is finding the whole process quite daunting.

Liam inherited a scheme of work from the outgoing teacher, but it was not very detailed, and his curriculum manager, Brenda, has given him some time to work on the planning of the upcoming sessions. Liam is finding the level of detail required to plan really challenging; the course is very demanding and the criteria for the course are explicit for each level of achievement (pass, merit and distinction). Liam is concerned that Brenda will want him to pitch all his sessions at 'distinction' level, as he knows the college is very aspirational, but he is concerned that – as a new teacher – he may let them down if he can't get everyone to work at that level.

Having studied the course requirements, Liam wants to use his first lesson to get to know his learners a bit better (as his predecessor completed the pre-course interviews), but knows time is at a premium. He compiles the following learning outcomes:

By the end of the lesson -

1. Learners will complete a self-assessment to provide the teacher with a clear view of prior learning
2. Learners will understand the course requirements and expectations
3. Learners will be able to re-cap the Level 2 requirements for Hospitality & Catering surrounding health and safety, and identify the additional demands of the Level 3
4. Learners will understand the homework requirements for a vocational personal statement introducing themselves for potential employers

As Liam has found, picking up a course can be quite demanding, especially a higher level course, but at least he has the right idea around setting clear objectives for the first lesson that will produce realistic outcomes. But how well has he composed them?

Consider the following:

1. Are all of those actually learning outcomes? Are there any included in Liam's list that may not qualify as learning outcomes? If so, which – and why?
2. Look at how some have been framed – 'understand', 'identify', 're-cap' – does this work, or can you find more appropriate ways of re-writing them?
3. Considering this is going to be his first session, can you identify any other potential learning outcomes that you would expect to see in the plan for a first session? What might you want to include in your first lesson as outcomes?

From the perspective of your observer, this is a really important feature, not only of how well you've planned your inclusive teaching and learning sessions, but also as a clear indicator for how well you are assessing progress; course criteria alone may not routinely be an evident feature of every session, but learning outcomes can be, and so with well-defined expectations, that are measurable, your observer can see with relative ease that you are monitoring their progress and are able to check, through your in-class assessment methods, on the levels of attainment.

Don't lose sight of the importance of checking learning in your sessions, and do capture those planned opportunities within your session plan. Not only is it the kind of good practice we would expect to see in any session, it is something you really want you observer to see when they come to assess you. Don't let yourself down by neglecting this.

Assessment requirements: understanding the internal and external needs in education

Requirements can vary from college to college, and indeed from awarding institution to awarding institution, so keeping up to date with these requirements is a part of the professional responsibility of the teacher. That said, there remain some fundamental easy wins that can be covered here, to at least kick-start you in the right direction.

Internal requirements – every provider or college will have very clear internal requirements, and this can – at times – seem like time-consuming record keeping. In fairness, when delivering accredited courses, much of the internal requirements will reflect these, so the bulk of external expectations around assessment we shall look at shortly.

Internal requirements are in place to support the organisation when executing its duty as an education provider and, as mentioned previously, education is much more like a business these days than perhaps it used to be. As such, the need for providers, especially those that are publicly funded (either in part or in its entirety), to be able to present auditable information, even on non-accredited courses, to demonstrate the value of learning. To be clear, the value of learning in this instance equates to learning actually taking place.

Within the last few years, the lack of any formal recording of achievements within courses that did not carry qualifications was a major cause for concern, and a lot of work was undertaken at how best to capture learning successes for participants on such courses. Recognising and recording progress and achievement (or RARPA, as it became known) remains a priority – and something that all teachers should be considering.

RARPA as a process was very clear that those all-important

starting points needed to be identified and recorded so that progress, or 'distance travelled,' could be determined on a learner-by-learner basis. Of course, a reliable initial assessment will provide this, but providing it in itself in not enough — it needs to be recorded somewhere, and then associated progress tracked.

The establishing of learning goals that are at overall course level, but also suitably individualised for your learners, is key to this, and most organisations will require this to be captured somewhere, usually documented as a record of that initial assessment. Similarly, links between the initial assessment and your planning need to be clear too (and this we shall cover later in this chapter), to demonstrate that you have used the information to inform your on-going planning.

Keeping records of progress, which may well be simple tracking sheets, or copies of written feedback, will also be key internal requirements, as it will form part of the audit process. But more than this — if you are collecting this information, so you can use it to make the learners' experiences the best they can have.

As mentioned at the very start of this section, every educational provider will differ in terms of what it wants and how it wants it, and sadly, as everyone is usually up against the clock, sometimes these are the things that can slip by at a teacher's induction. As a professional, take the lead — seek out the answers for yourself, approach your line manager and ask what (if any) documentation they require. It may be digital, it may follow specific guidelines; take ownership of needing to find out so that you can do the best job possible. Also, this ensures you're not waiting for an internal observer to pick you up on missing something. As is often the case, ignorance is no defence!

External requirements — now, some of these will undoubtedly overlap with internal requirements, because in many cases, providers tend to adopt models of accredited assessment practice for their non-accredited provision to ensure the quality is consistently high and that processes around assessment are robust.

Like internal requirements, of course, different external bodies will have different processes and specific requirements so the rule about checking for local expectations remains on your shoulders. That said, there are always going to be some very clear external requirements that all awarding bodies will expect.

Clearly recorded initial assessment records that demonstrate the entry points for the learners on the course, ideally with the learners' individual registration numbers once they are assigned (and their registration date with the awarding body), are essential. This is really important – increasingly, awarding organisations such as City & Guilds, Northern College of Further Education (NCFE), Pearson, EdExcel and others have increased vigilance around learners being formally assessed before they have been registered with them as 'live' learners. This can lead to providers having their official status with the awarding organisation put into jeopardy – please, please be mindful of this and plan your formal assessment strategy to allow for it.

Formative assessment tracking is also very important to these external agencies, and the recording of progress against the course criteria, the specific goals of individuals, and key performance milestones is essential. Never has the term 'audit' been more appropriate, as that is what the awarding institution needs to be able to do. It is their reputation at stake when their qualifications are being handed out and they need to have confidence in the provider, and the course teacher, that assessment against their standards is rigorous. So, when your observer needs to see you are meeting external requirements, you need to be able to have this readily available for them.

Something else that will be of concern to the external

organisations that you may well also wish to keep within your teaching file would be minutes from team meetings (where you'll also have been communicating with other learning professionals). Minutes of meetings are excellent evidence of your meeting of external requirements (as well as internal ones, come to that) as meetings will also occasionally feature standardisation activity.

Standardisation is a process also sometimes referred to as moderation, whereby those in the delivery team work together under the leadership of either an internal quality verifier (role titles vary from organisation to organisation) or the curriculum manager, and revisit the marking of assignments, or other course work, against standards to ensure that all staff using those standards have a shared understanding of what is acceptable – and what is not – at the various levels being delivered. This also helps ensure that the teachers are conforming to the reliability aspect of the principles of assessment; awarding organisations need to have confidence that teachers are all applying the same criteria in the same way and, to be fair, so too do the learners.

Written feedback is very important in supporting learners to improve. Feedback should not only celebrate the successful elements of a learner's work, but also be completely clear and transparent about what the learners need to do to continue to improve, or in the event they have not met the requirements at this point, detailed guidance on how to meet the criteria upon a further submission. On qualification courses, it is a requirement of awarding bodies that part of the quality process includes samples of the learners' work are subject to internal verification, and this is a process whereby the teachers' marking is scrutinised to ensure the marking is compliant with the principles of assessment, and is fair, proportionate and appropriate for the work provided. Copies of feedback to learners should be kept for your observer to also sample.

Appeals procedures are important, as the learners have a right to access this in the event that they disagree with the marking of their work, for example. These are both local (provider-specific) and external (and vary by awarding organisation), but should be communicated to the learners early in the course, and a copy of the process should be available. Again, this may well be something that you consider including in your teaching file.

The final key external agency to consider that sits outside of awarding institutions is our old friend, Ofsted. As a governmentally appointed regulator of quality standards in education, Ofsted is always going to be keen to examine the quality and rigour of assessment, both in terms of undertaking assessment, and also in terms of the effectiveness of recording individuals' progress. If the teacher is unaware how well learners are progressing, then how can they ensure the learners know, and indeed, that they know how to improve? Ofsted will be looking to confirm that learners do know, and can articulate it.

REALITY CHECK:

Routinely self-auditing your assessment records may not be a bad idea, not least to ensure you are being thorough in supporting your learners.

1. *Review how you are capturing and recording your initial assessment findings. What information have you actually compiled, and how have you used it?*
2. *What are you using to track progress? It is transparent? Could a peer look at your records and understand at-a-glance what it tells them? Could an observer? Could it be clearer?*

Adaptable assessment? Demonstrating your flexible approach

As with all aspects of the teaching, learning and assessment cycle, flexibility is a key feature of a good teacher's skillset. Of course, how flexibility manifests itself can, and will, vary greatly from course to course. What is important, is that as the teacher, you are very aware of what you can do to ensure that assessment is as accessible as possible, without compromising the authenticity of the process.

Where assessment is concrete, due to the external nature of the qualification, it may be you have limited scope to be flexible in terms of your formal assessment. As discussed, if learners do have additional needs, then communicating with the Exams and/or the Inclusion Officer may provide some opportunities to be flexible to ensure fair access, and if so ensure you have a record of this in your teaching file for your observer to see. However, more organically, you can demonstrate flexibility through some more informal classroom assessment, irrespective of whether the course leads to a qualification or not.

Using effective verbal questioning techniques cannot be underestimated as an informal assessment method that can be easily adapted through your use of your own English language minimum core skills. Learners need questions to be adequately differentiated for them, and you can do this. However, going a step further, you can be flexible in how you approach this as you identify learners may struggle, at times, with how they are phrased. Being able to rephrase questions, for example, to make them more accessible, is an easy way to demonstrate flexibility – and probably something you do on a regular basis.

It is very common for trainee-teachers to worry that they need to cram lots of grandstanding into the sessions to meet criteria – the reality is you simply need to do your job as you normally would: well.

Making assessment matter: using the data to drive up achievement

Capturing assessment data is a vital element of the assessment process. Without it, and without you using it, the assessments themselves are pretty pointless. Why? Because, if we're honest, assessment isn't just to tick boxes. Assessment is the key tool that really helps us to help our learners to improve.

The information we glean from conducting our assessments provides us with several opportunities, and this last section of the chapter will look at these opportunities, bringing home the fact, I hope, that only by using the outcomes of your assessments, can you really make a difference through your teaching sessions.

Opportunity one: the initial assessment. This very first assessment phase allows you to support the learners in the development of suitable individualised targets, or milestones, to help structure and inform their own learning pathway with you. But not only this, as the data you capture here should, and in fact must, inform your initial planning. Not to labour the point (although, I probably am), this is a prime example of how you need to use the information you generate or else the whole initial assessment is a waste.

By having a clear overview of your entire cohort via the initial assessment data, you know already (more or less) levels of ability, confidence, prior knowledge and skills and you can already begin to revise and adapt your scheme of work, and certainly your early session plans. Don't forget, you may have planned the structure and skeleton of your course way in advance of meeting your learners, but now you can add some of the flesh to those bones; now you know, to some extent, your learners, and so you can begin to vary elements of complexity or demand to ensure all of those learners are being effectively stretched and challenged based on your starting point. Handily, this leads us to...

Opportunity two: Differentiated learning. Naturally, by consolidating your initial assessment data you can determine how best to provide levels of support, and indeed levels of less support, to effectively ensure a differentiated learning experience as far as is possible. This can also include the referencing of individual targets and goals within sessions, to make explicit links to that which learners are keen to explore. This again is extremely valuable for your observer to witness, as it can demonstrate several skills. As ever, make everyone's life easier, and ensure your session plan clearly details how you are doing this, as it may not be obvious from your seamless delivery how you are meeting those needs.

Opportunity three: Feeding back. A key outcome from your assessment is the provision of feedback to learners. Without feedback, assessment is just a chore for learners that they really won't appreciate. Your marking of their work, or your observation of their skills in action; whatever assessment looks like in your classes, it provides you as the expert the necessary information to allow you to feed back – and this is so significant.

Feeding back can take many forms. It can be informal, verbal feedback, or it can by through peers if there has been a peer assessment activity. Often the most tangibly valuable is written feedback, from their teacher, that takes the time to recognise the good work they have completed, and identifying their strengths, but also being constructive in its acknowledgement of any areas for improvement. Learners are attending your class because they want to be better. As discussed, they actually want to be able to do it without you, ultimately, so they need that feedback, and they need it to keep them motivated, but still focus upon what they can do better. Vague comments are no use here – you are being employed to provide meaningful feedback that learners themselves can use. If they can't articulate what it is they need to do to improve, then the feedback has failed. That isn't their fault; that fault is the teacher's.

Opportunity four: tracking progress. Through the collection of formative assessment data, whether it is against set criteria or personal targets, it is possible for the teacher to monitor the pace of attainment, and through this, the effectiveness of their own delivery. Using assessment information to, in part at least, inform the evaluation of a teaching session or, on a grander scale, a whole course, can be invaluable. After all, if one or two learners aren't keeping up, or don't progress at the same pace as others that can be perfectly normal. If the whole class seems to be under-performing, this could be indicative of some other issues, and those issues may be the teacher's. You can see how assessment data can be extremely useful to the teacher, and the learners, on several levels.

So with the close of this chapter, we have fittingly finally covered all of the mandatory assessment criteria for your observed teaching practice assessments. Depending on some of the other units you may have to do, which in itself is dependent upon where you are undertaking your teaching qualification, there may be unit-specific criteria you also need to meet, such as using resources in your specialist subject, or promoting English, maths and employability skills, but remember this – applying the principles covered in this book so far will stand you in good stead. Look at that extra criteria and consider what you are already doing; chances are you'll be meeting those standards, or can be with very little adaptation.

The next chapter will explore post-observation reflection, and how to move forwards following each of your observations, maximising the use of the feedback, and indeed building on everything we have addressed, to make each subsequent observation even more successful, and ensuring you are as prepared as possible for your next observation. Congratulations – you're nearly there!

6 REFLECTION AS ACTION

This chapter will explore two main strands for you to consider; firstly, it will contemplate how best to respond following your observation, and how you can approach, and make effective use of, the feedback that you have received. Secondly, we can reflect on everything we have discussed in the book thus far, with a view to enabling you to pro-actively prepare for your next and subsequent observations.

This chapter relates to the following Professional Standards:

Professional values and attributes – (1) Evaluate what works best in your teaching and learning to meet the diverse needs of your learners; (2) Evaluate and challenge your practice, values and beliefs; (3) Inspire, motivate and raise expectations for learners through your enthusiasm and knowledge; (4) Be creative and innovative in selecting and adapting strategies to help learners to learn; (5) Value and promote social and cultural diversity, equality of opportunity and inclusion; (6) Build positive and collaborative relationships with colleagues and learners

Professional knowledge and understanding – (7) Maintain and update knowledge of your subject and/or vocational area; (9) Apply theoretical understanding of effective practice in teaching, learning and assessment drawing on research and other evidence; (10) Evaluate your practice with others to assess its impact on learning; (11); Manage and promote positive learner behaviour; (12) Understand the teaching and professional role and your responsibilities

Professional skills – (13) Motivate and inspire learners to promote achievement and develop their skills to enable progression; (14) Plan and deliver effective learning programmes for diverse groups; (15) Promote the benefits of technology and support learners in its use; (16) Address the mathematics and English needs of learners, and work creatively to overcome individual barriers to learning; (17) Enable learners to share responsibility for their own learning and assessment, setting goals that stretch and challenge; (18) Apply appropriate and fair methods of assessment and provide constructive and timely feedback to support progression and achievement; (20) Contribute to organisational development and quality improvement through collaboration with others

We have now explored all of the core mandatory criteria for your teaching practice assessed observations, although (as mentioned in Chapter 5) there may be additional, unit specific, criteria depending on the units being used by your teacher-training provider.

This means that the emphasis for preparation now rests entirely with you. Well, almost entirely. There are still a couple of tricks up the proverbial sleeve that may yet come in handy for you as you engage with your assessed observations.

One of the biggest post-observation pitfalls that trainees stumble into is engaging meaningfully with the feedback provided by their observer. So, before we go back to the start, let's spend a few moments looking at that most overlooked aspect of observations – what happens once it's over.

Reflection is your friend: identifying key messages

For many trainees, surviving the classroom observation is enough for them. Getting through it and not failing is their main goal. This can be as a result of nerves, or a lack of confidence in their own ability, or it could be due to simply not caring about the feedback – just getting through it, for them, is fine.

Actually, it isn't.

Coasting isn't good enough in this age of continuous improvement, and this particularly applies to the standards required of professional teachers. As with your own learners, you provide feedback to both acknowledge what it is they have done well, but also, and possibly more significantly, what they still need to develop. Your assessed observation works in much the same way. Whilst different awarding organisations may lay out the observation report form differently, the components are a constant, so let's think about these.

Confirmation of meeting performance standards – the observer is required to confirm (a) that you have completed specific criteria, but also (b) **how** you have. This, therefore, is very heavily dependent on your observer having access to evidence that will facilitate these confirmations. This will be, primarily, through observing your skills in action, but also through a review of the key documentation that demonstrates some of the other aspects of the standards to be met. The onus is on you to make sure this is clear, well-organised, and easy to follow.

Summary of performance – depending on the awarding institution, the report may include an overall summary, usually broken down into key elements (such as *'planning,' 'delivery,' 'communication,' 'resources,' 'assessment,'* and *'feedback.'*). This is an executive summary of the criteria being confirmed and a distillation for your benefit of the key findings of the observer.

You shouldn't be finding anything in this section that doesn't appear in the main body of the report but, more importantly, this section provides more of a fluid narrative that pulls the themes emerging through the confirmation of the criteria section for your attention.

Key Strengths – rather speaks for itself, this section allows the observer to highlight the clear strengths for the session that they feel need to be flagged up for recognition. Sometimes, trainees worry that there aren't that many strengths, especially over their first few observations. Don't panic about this, after all, in the first instance you are still learning and growing and, assuming you do make use of the feedback provided to improve, then you should see these increase. In the second instance, strengths should be those aspects of your delivery that are above and beyond what is normally expected in a session. Remember – standards are high, and a lot of 'good practice' may well be considered a 'norm.' Therefore, 'norms' are unlikely to appear as strengths in your report.

Key Areas for Improvement – the ying to the previous point's yang, this is possibly the most important part of the observation feedback but, perhaps understandably, it is also the element many trainees shy away from. No-one really enjoys having shortcomings pointed out to them, especially if it is about our professional work, but don't lose sight of why the observer is telling you this; they are trying to enable you to improve, and so to be the best you can. The areas for improvement can often seem lengthy in comparison with the strengths, and this is often particularly true early in your observation cycle, but this is pretty much to be expected. This is a learning mechanism, and how you engage with it will define your approach to personal development as much as it will your attitude to teaching, and we'll consider this in a little more detail in a moment.

Agreed Action Plan – usually the final section of the observation report, the action plan draws on the areas for improvement and – ideally, but not always – a discussion with you to set out the next steps you need to take, and the actions you need to take prior to the next observation. Again, this is not to knock your confidence and your esteem, it is there to provide you with a developmental scaffolding on which you can build your specific improvements.

The key messages from the observer are there, not to bring you down or demoralise you (that's not the reason you give developmental feedback to your learners, is it?), but rather to highlight to you the areas that require a little more thought, and a little more attention. This feedback is invaluable, and accepting it is all a matter of attitude.

Attitude hasn't really been a feature of this book, but as you'll have noticed from the professional standards that open every chapter, having a professional attitude that is open to continually improving, and collaborating with others in order to do so, is front and centre. Self-reflection and evaluation can be really useful, but it is a very limited frame of reference. Think about the potential for improvement when you are open to the thoughts, experiences and suggestions of other, more experienced, educational professionals. The possibilities are limitless.

This isn't just an attitude that will see you through your training as a teacher, but one that will also carry you forwards into your professional career. Even the most dynamic, confident and experienced teachers love the opportunity of liaising with others to share unexpected issues they've encountered (there's always another one of those around the corner, no matter how long you've been teaching, believe me), and to grow from it as a professional. But you do need to want to improve, and you need to not hide from the areas of improvement, but own them, accept them and then use them.

Putting reflection into action: a couple of approaches to applying feedback for improvement

Once you have accepted that there are areas for improvement, you can start to determine how best to tackle them. Let's get this clear – not tackling them is really not an option for you. You may not necessarily agree with everything that your observer has identified, but look beyond that. Can you, dispassionately (which isn't easy, I appreciate), look at those areas for improvement and see where the observer is coming from?

It may well be that they are not looking at it from your perspective, as the teacher, but instead from the perspective of the impact on the learners. It could be that they are making recommendations to help you develop your use of assessment and tracking, to ensure you are as robust as the sector demands. If in doubt, read through the 'confirmation' section of the report, as you shouldn't find anything in the *Key Areas for Improvement* that are not flagged up under the criteria sections as being in need of some kind of development. If you still feel unclear, then go back to your observer for clarity – you are the learner in this context, after all, and learners have the right to seek clarification.

Taking this forwards, once you have recognised the improvement needed, there are many ways to then work with this. Here, let us look at two possible approaches to taking the feedback and applying it to your own practice in such a way that you can then take pro-active steps to address the issues raised, and in turn improve your own delivery and overall effectiveness for the future. A final point for clarification is not to get too hung up on the application of the areas for improvement, or the actions, to the session as it was that was observed. That lesson has now gone, and will never come back. Even if you deliver the same course in the future, that lesson has gone. Next time, you'll have different learners on a different day, with different skills, so a literal application is almost a pointless exercise.

Observers fully appreciate that the session they observed will never, truly be repeated, and their feedback isn't just for that session, so please don't see it in such narrow terms. The feedback is constructed to ensure that you can apply new and different thinking to any and all future sessions. You'll waste time and energy if you only think of applying the adjustments to that specific session; these are suggestions for you to apply to all of your delivery, where applicable. Think bigger picture, always.

Practice & Process – This is one approach to engaging with your feedback, and can help you to really focus in on what is required. Firstly, review the range of areas for improvement and the actions proposed.

Now, categorise them as either 'process-linked' or 'practice-linked' (it may help to produce two lists to support you in this activity). Once you have done this, you can look at exactly how best to implement the changes. Let's consider what might come up under 'practice-linked' areas for improvement:

- *Pace of the lesson too fast/slow for too many learners*
- *Insufficiently individualised differentiation for higher ability learners*
- *Under-developed use of questioning techniques to stimulate and monitor learning*
- *Missed opportunities to effectively use resources to promote equality*
- *Insufficiently learner-centred activity to fully support participation and inclusion*
- *Poor communication between the teacher and the learners, with frequent spelling and grammatical errors in written materials*
- *Insufficient attention to correcting learners' English in their written work*

This is just a smattering of some of the most regularly recurring areas for improvement, but of course it is far from an exhaustive list. This is merely designed to be indicative of some of the areas that can crop up through observation feedback.

'Process-linked' improvement areas could look like this:

- *Insufficiently detailed lesson plan to fully structure and manage the range of activities, and differing ability levels*
- *No links between session outcomes or content and individual goals*
- *Under-developed recording of initial assessment results to effectively inform planning*
- *Inadequate setting of learner goals*
- *Inconsistent tracking of learners' progress and achievement*
- *Poor attention to organisational safeguarding requirements*

Again, far from exhaustive, but as an approach this helps you to divide and conquer those areas for improvement into manageable chunks.

Process driven improvements tend to be related to your documentation, or the internal (and external) requirements for curriculum, or assessment, not being adhered to fully. In many respects, these can be the quickest fixes for you to tackle first. Look at what the observer's feedback is telling you is missing, or under-developed. It is often the case, especially early in the teacher training course, that the ground work has been laid by the teacher, but because of trying to juggle all of the demands around them, they don't quite dot all the 'i's and cross all the 't's. This feedback is ideal, then, to help highlight these aspects, and affords you the opportunity to tidy up the procedural bits so you can divert your attention to the planning and the delivery.

Extended Action Planning – this is an approach that requires you to go slightly further than the agreed actions provided by your observer, and actually take the key messages from the report and convert it into an auditable plan that you can also track your own progress against. Another added advantage to this approach is that you can include your extended action plan in your teaching folder for your observer, so they can see exactly how you are taking their feedback on board, and using it.

There are, of course, many different approaches you can adopt for your action plan, but for ease, I'd suggest the following format, as it is easy for you to maintain, and very clear to monitor:

	Adjustments Required	Impact(s) on learners	Date Implemented	Additional adjustments?
Area for Improvement				

Simple to replicate, this action plan allows you to chart all of the key features of any areas for improvement that you have been presented with.

Your observer-identified areas for improvement are inserted into the left hand column, and you can then list the implied adjustments you need to put into place in the next column. This could be as simple as a single action, or it may be a list of three or four key actions.

The next column allows you to reconcile the areas for improvement – and the associated actions you are taking as a result – with the positive impact it will have on your learners. This is important to recognise, as if there is ultimately no positive impact on the learners, one would question the nature of the area for improvement. After all, even the inclusion of process-driven areas for improvement should still link to improved learner experiences. Also, once you can make these links, the improvements themselves tend to become a little more logical.

Following this, you can easily determine (and record) when you intend to have implemented these changes, either collectively or action by action, depending what is most appropriate and possible. There is no mileage in being unrealistic with your actions here, as you'll only get bogged down, stressed out and ultimately disengaged. Take control, and set realistic timeframes in which to work.

Lastly, you have scope to recognise that – having implemented your adjustments – more may be required as a result. This demonstrates your own evaluative and reflective skills in action, and helps support your own professional continuous improvement. Using a couple from the mocked up lists cited earlier, I've completed two rows as an example for you.

Clearly, there is no 'one true way' for you tackle any given identified areas for improvement, and a range of factors may influence what you can, or cannot, actually do. For example, your subject, where you teach, the nature of your learners – all of these, and more – can bring additional hurdles for you to overcome. Excitingly, this isn't something that will go away once you gain your qualification. If anything, you may even become more exposed to these kinds of wider issues, and the expectation that you'll respond positively and manage each new situation won't ever diminish. Welcome to the teaching profession!

Let's have a look at these areas for improvement. The first two are completed, but what might you include if you were confronted with the third one? How would you action plan your improvements?

Surviving The Classroom Observation

Area for Improvement	Adjustments Required	Impact(s) on learners	Date Implemented	Additional adjustments?
Insufficiently individualised differentiation for higher ability learners	1. Ensure that the IA record is up to date 2. Include activities to stretch higher level learners, including extended questions, within the classes 3. Record this on my session plans	All learners are able to engage at a level suitably challenging for them. Having this recorded on the session plan will remind me to deploy regularly nominated questions to routinely stretch and challenge as the opportunity arises.	14th Nov (next session)	1. Enhance my IA record to include more information that will support me in challenging learners at both ends of the ability spectrum.
Inconsistent tracking of learners' progress and achievement	1. Ensure all of my tracking sheets are prepared, up-to-date, and include learners' targets 2. Update after every session.	I will be able to ensure pace of sessions is appropriate to learners' capacity for attainment. Feedback to learners can draw on their charted progress.	14th Nov (Next session)	N/A
Insufficient correcting of learners' English errors in their written work				

As mentioned, these are simply two of many different ways you can approach the implementation of your feedback, following your observed assessment. Neither are officially prescribed, but what is important is that you do implement something.

Your observer will not be impressed if, upon returning to observe you following a few weeks, that some key records have not been updated (indeed, it sends quite a signal about your commitment as a teacher to both your own development, but also your commitment to the course itself). How would you feel if your learners disregarded your feedback, and continued – in your eyes – to make the same mistakes repeatedly? Frustrated, I imagine, to say the least.

What can be even more frustrating to observers is something that here and now you may well think is a little absurd, but believe me it is far from it. That is something I shall refer to now as 'feedback amnesia' although I daresay observers may well have more colourful terms for it! Feedback amnesia is the condition trainee teachers sometimes manifest around their third, fourth and fifth observations, and is a phenomenon that really can work against them.

As you may have guessed, this refers to the unhelpful knee-jerk quick fixing of areas for improvement identified only in the previous observation, and utterly disregarding any prior changes that were requested (and made) in light of addressing new issues. This is not a sign of personal development, more that actions taken are to appease the observer rather than to improve one's own practice fundamentally. Observers having to give feedback that re-treads aspects of delivery that had previously been addressed is not something you want to be encouraging. Using something like the action plan format allows you to add rows with every observation, rather than starting over, so you are always reminded of what you have been guided to act upon, and never loose sight of it.

Forewarned is forearmed: putting your learning into practice

So, we have covered the observation criteria and what to do with your feedback once you have received it, as well as the importance of not slipping back into old habits; make it an aim to never get the same areas for improvement twice.

Now the task falls to you to take everything that we have discussed and explored, and use it to prepare for your observations. Perhaps you have already had one, or perhaps you are yet to experience your first one – either way, you have all the information you need to make the next observation (and all subsequent observations) a success. As with any good assessment, you are clear on what you are being assessed on, as it is all in the observation report form which you will have seen, and which have all been covered within these pages. There are no surprises.

However, you are still able to do more. You can reflect upon all of those mandatory criteria, and determine what you could ensure is included in your session, either in your delivery or in your teaching folder as evidence, to meet the requirements that your observer is there to see.

This is a very straightforward activity, and as with anything, there are many ways you could go about preparing yourself, but for my part, I'd advocate using the observation criteria as a checklist of sorts, to focus your mind on those features of your teaching, learning and assessment practices that will be under the microscope for the duration of the observed session, as well as any supportive materials and documentation that you know your observer will need to see to validate that you have met certain standards.

To make your life easier, you could use the following to map this out:

Criteria	How will this be observed?	Documentary evidence available?
Confirm how the candidate has designed teaching and learning plans which respond to a) the individual goals and needs of all learners; and b) curriculum requirements		
Confirm how the candidate has established and sustained a safe inclusive learning environment		
Confirm how the candidate has used inclusive teaching and learning approaches and resources, including technologies, to meet the individual needs of learners		
Confirm how the candidate has demonstrated ways to promote equality and value diversity in own teaching		
Confirm how the candidate has communicated with learners and learning professionals to meet individual learning needs and encourage progression		

Confirm how the candidate has used types and methods of assessment including peer and self-assessment to: *a) involve learners in assessment* *b) meet the individual needs of learners* *c) enable learners to produce assessment evidence that is reliable, sufficient, authentic and* *d) meet current internal and external assessment requirements*		
Confirm how the candidate has applied minimum core elements in planning, delivering and assessing inclusive teaching and learning		
Confirm how the candidate has designed resources that actively promote *a) equality and value diversity; and* *b) meet the identified needs of specific learners*		
Confirm how the candidate has demonstrated flexibility and adaptability in the use in the use of inclusive teaching and learning approaches		

and resources, including technologies, to meet the needs of individual learners		
Confirm how the candidate has demonstrated flexibility and adaptability in using types and methods of assessment to meet individual learning needs and assessment requirements		
Confirm how the candidate has used assessment data in: a) monitoring learners' achievement, attainment and progress b) setting learners' targets c) planning subsequent sessions; and d) recording the outcomes of assessment		

You can use this to act as an aide memoir when it comes to planning your sessions in anticipation of an observed assessment. This is not to say that you need to put on a show, as such, but it makes perfect sense that you prepare well for your formal assessment. Make use of this advantage, and ensure that you seize every opportunity to present your skills and knowledge through your delivery, as well as your teaching folder, so that you can confidently deliver your sessions without worrying about that person sitting in the corner testing you. Remember, if you are prepared, tests aren't really all that scary after all.

7 ONE STEP CLOSER: FINAL THOUGHTS

This chapter wraps up the key points from this book, and plants a few final seeds for you to consider as your practice develops, and also that may help you continue to mature and grow as a member of the teaching profession.

We should never lose sight of the fact that these observations are tests. Of course, they are tests designed to make you better as a professional teacher, and to encourage the development of administrative habits that will support your work, and in doing so support you in nurturing your learners through all aspects of teaching, learning and assessment. But they are tests.

This book, in many ways, represents a revision guide for you to prepare for these tests, but it is hoped that along the way it offers you more than just the way to demonstrate you can, and have, met the standards expected of you. It is hoped that some of the activities will encourage you to think about your delivery, about your planning and approach to assessing. It is hoped that you don't feel these pages have merely 'taught to the test' but instead have opened your mind to consider a range of ways to tackle the array of issues you will encounter in your ongoing work as a professional teacher. That has always certainly been the intention, although of course it does need to support you through those observations (crazy if it didn't, after all).

But now we are here, in the final few pages, I wanted to take a moment or two to consider the last few developmental opportunities that are available to you, that possibly sit outside the obvious boundaries of the observed teaching practice assessments, but are nevertheless valuable considerations for you, moving forwards.

After all, this process is designed to equip you not just for today, but also for the future. To do this well, you need to be able to go forwards independently and continue to grow and develop way beyond the final date of your teacher-training course.

Mentioned a few times within these pages is the fabled 'teacher folder – something that you can present as part of your observation as the repository of much (if not all) of your documentary evidence. The file may be something that forms part of the internal requirements for your institution, or it may be something that you put together to support you in compartmentalising and organising your teaching documents.

The folder can be a really useful tool for teachers, new or otherwise, in keeping key aspects of their work together, and accessible for those who need to audit it.

The folder could contain:

Your scheme of work
Your session plans (most recent first)
Your initial assessment records
Your formative tracking sheets (including learner goals)
Any communication regarding learners with specific needs
Individual learning plans, if you use these

I'm sure you can also identify other things that you may benefit from keeping in the folder. A working document in itself, keeping it up to date helps you not only ensure your records are maintained, but with every observation (whether for your teacher training or as part of the internal quality monitoring cycle of your organisation) you can be confident that your observer can see how you assess, plan and the rationale behind any differentiation, as well as how you are supporting those with any identified support needs.

Liaising with your peers is also a very important part of your own professional growth as a teacher. The amassed experiences that you can access, whether through team meetings, or by arranging online forums (even a dedicated social media group, perhaps) to allow you to converse professionally, is invaluable. Given how often time is at a premium for us all, face to face communication – whilst ideal – can be hard to schedule. Making use of the available technologies can really support you, and help you not feel you are working in isolation.

Taking this a step further, I'd also like to recommend that you consider the use of peer observations as a professional development tool; observation has long been in place as a mechanism to promote improvement whilst also assuring quality, but at its heart, it is a tool rooted in professionalism. A few colleges do offer peer observation schemes as part of the continuous professional development opportunities they provide, but even where these are not routinely available, it may be worth exploring with your line manager.

What we can gain from observing the work of another, especially if they are an experienced and celebrated teacher of good standing, can be immeasurable. Seeing how they manage the class, how they differentiate (possibly how they record it on the session plan, even), how they use innovative approaches to stimulate and nurture learning; seeing this in action, without any pressure on you to perform, can be a very valuable developmental activity.

> **REALITY CHECK:**
>
> *Consider observing an experienced teacher*
>
> *What will you be focusing on? Classroom management? Effective use of resources? Monitoring progress and achievement? Diversity?*
>
> *Devise a report form that will allow you to capture all the aspects you think you need to observe, as it will be very useful when you observe.*

Of course, your organisation will probably offer much in the way of continuing professional development, and you would be well advised to take these opportunities. A good teacher never stops learning, and there will always be new ideas, new ways of working and, inevitably, new layers of expectation as policy changes on a national level. It is your job to keep on top of these changes, so that you can be as current and effective as you can be.

I hope this collection of thoughts and ideas has helped you in some small way to feel more confident in addressing the issues of observed teaching practice, and in doing so has helped you feel able to embrace the assessment for what it is – an opportunity to be the best you can, and a chance to find out how to be even better.

Good luck with you teacher training, and may you have many happy sessions ahead of you.

BIBLIOGRAPHY

Bernstein, B. (1996), "Discourses, Knowledge Structures and Fields: Some Arbitrary Considerations," Taylor Francis, INC.

Bratchell, D.F. (1968), "The Aims and Organisation of Further Education," Bath: Pergamon.

Bristow, A (1970) "Inside Colleges of Further Education," London: DES/HMSO.

Bruner, J (1960) "The Process of Education." USA: Harvard University Press

Cantor, L., Roberts, I. (1986), "Further Education Colleges Today: A Critical Review, (3rd Ed)." London: Routledge and Kegan Paul.

Crowther Report, (1959) "15-18: A Report for the Central Advisory Council for Education" London: HMSO.

DfES (2005) "Equipping our Teachers of the Future: Reforming Initial Teacher Training for the Learning and Skills Sector," London: DfES

DfES (2005a) "Initial Teacher Training – Making the Reforms Happen," London; DfES

FENTO (2004) "Addressing language, literacy and numeracy needs in education and training: defining the minimum core of teachers' knowledge, understanding and personal skill – a guide for initial teacher education programmes," London; FENTO

FENTO (2004a) "Including Language, literacy and Numeracy Learning in all Post-16 Education: guidance on curriculum and methodology for generic ITE programmes," London; FENTO

Foden, F. (1992) "The Education of Part-time Teachers in Further and Adult Education," London: Further Education Unit.

Foster Report (2005), "Realising the Potential: A review of the future role of further education colleges," Department for Education and Skills; London: DfES

Gibbs, G. (1988), "Learning by Doing: a guide to teaching and learning methods." Oxford: Further Education Unit.

Gleeson, D; Mardle, G. (1980) "Further Education or Training?" London: Routledge and Kegan Paul.

Gravells, A (2011) "Principles and Practice of Assessment in the Lifelong Learning Sector," Exeter: Learning Matters

Guile, D., Lucas, N. (1999), "Rethinking Initial Teacher Education and Professional Development in Further Education," London: Institute of Education, University of London.

Hobley, J (2005) "Institutionally Focused Study: Doctorate in Education," Institute of Education, London. Unpublished.

James Report (1972), "Teacher Training and Education," London: HMSO

Lucas, N (2004), "Teaching in Further Education: New Perspectives for a Changing Context," London: Institute of Education, University of London.

McNair Report (1944), "Teachers and Youth Leaders," Board of Education, London: HMSO

O'Connor, D (2004) "7407 – Introducing the Common Core"; City and

Guilds of London Institute workshop; Unpublished.

OFSTED (2003), "The Initial Training of Further Education Teachers: A Survey," London, HMI 1762

OFSTED (2004), "Handbook for the inspection of initial training of further education teachers," HMI 2275

Purdie, D (2002), "Issues, Policies and Values: Building Esteem in Non-traditional Learners," Certificate in Education, University of Greenwich. Unpublished.

Purdie, D (2011) 'The Good, The Bad & The Uninformed: An Exploration of what Good or Better Teaching Looks Like Within The FE Sector" Institute of Education, London

Raffe, D (1994), "The Third Face of Modules," Journal of Education and Work, volume 7 (3).

Russell Report (1966), "The Supply and Training of Teachers for Further Education," Department for Education and Science; London: HMSO

Willis Jackson Report (1957), "The Supply and Training of Teachers for Technical Colleges," Report of Special Committee, Ministry of Education, London: HMSO.

Young, M., Lucas, N., Sharp, G. and Cunningham, B. (1995), "Teacher Education for the Further Education Sector: Training the Lecturer of the Future," Report produced for the Association of Colleges by Post-16 Centre. London: Institute of Education, University of London.

SPECIAL THANKS

A number of trainee-teachers contributed directly to the research that informed several aspects of this book, and I'd very much like to acknowledge them here for their participation:

Bradley Burton, Elisa Cantwell, Marta Cappellini, Ruben Choque, Peter Dunn, Leeana Fitzpatrick, Raul Guerrero, Lorraine Hooper, Matthew Hughes, Annick Janganant, Sasha Martin, Keeley Marsh, Jessica Mills, Allison Pidgeon, Gina Saggers, Jon Smith, Shereen Tracey, Andrea Turner, Nichola Turpin, Elizabeth Walsh & Mia Warwick

Similarly, I wish to thank the observers I have the luxury of working regularly with, who provided me with much insight into the challenges faced and on both sides of the observation:

*Alexander Dunitz, Brenda Hunt, Vedia Mustafa,
and particularly Joanne Mead for editorial support*

Lastly I wish to thank the many colleges who have invited me inside to work with their observers and assessors and teaching staff. Whilst I am there in a supporting and developing role, I never fail to feel enriched myself by the often excellent teaching and learning I find.

Printed in Great Britain
by Amazon